We have taken great pleasure in drawing up
Secret Edinburgh and hope that through its
guidance you will, like us, continue to discover
unusual, hidden or little-known aspects of the city.
Descriptions of certain places are accompanied
by thematic sections highlighting historical details
or anecdotes as an aid to understanding the city
in all its complexity.
Secret Edinburgh also draws attention to
the multitude of details found in places that
we may pass every day without noticing.
These are an invitation to look more closely at
the urban landscape and, more generally,
a means of seeing our own city with the curiosity
and attention that we often display while
travelling elsewhere …

f **secretunusualedinburgh**

▸ **@secret_unusual**

◉ **@secret_unusual**

Comments on this guide and its contents, as well as
information on sites not mentioned, are welcome
and will help us to enrich future editions.
Don't hesitate to contact us:
• Jonglez Publishing,
  17, boulevard du Roi,
  78000 Versailles, France
• E-mail: info@jonglezpublishing.com

NB: all buses are run by Lothian unless specified otherwise

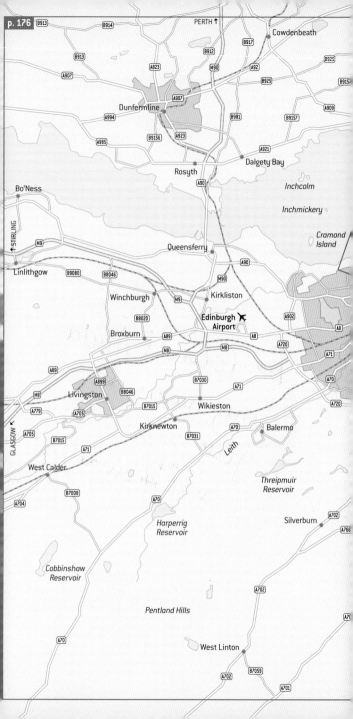
PERTH ↑

p. 92
p. 56
p. 14
p. 134
p. 20

0   5   10 km

N

A910
A921
Kirkcaldy
B925
B9157
A921
Kinghorn
urntisland

Firth of Forth

Inchkeith

Aberlady
A198
Spittal
Port of Leith
Cockenzie and Port Seton
B1348
Longniddry
Prestonpans
A198
EDINBURGH
Musselburgh
B1348
A1
Tranent
A199
A199
B6363
A6093
B6414
B6355
B6371
A6093
Ormiston
Pencaitland
A6106
A772
A7
A720
A6124
A68
Dalkeith
A6106
A720
A701
A768
Bonnyrigg
Loanhead
A702 A703
A7
Newtongrange
A6093
Pathhead
A6371
Roslin
Rosewell
B6372
Humbie
B7026
Gorebridge
B6367
Fala
Penicuik
A6458
A68
01
B6372
A7
B6367
A6094
B6372
B7007
A703
B709
A7
B6368
Gladhouse
Reservoir
B7007
Portmore
Reservoir
Moorfoot Hills

CONTENTS

WEST

CONTENTS

EAST

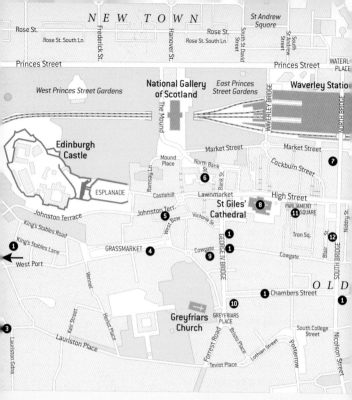

OLD TOWN

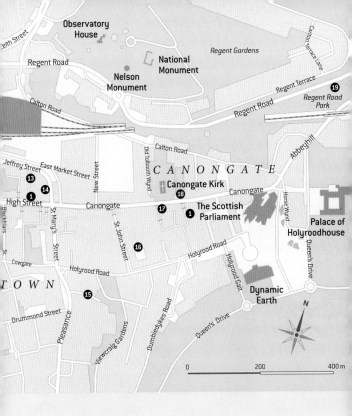

MYSTERIOUS EDINBURGH BOOK SCULPTURES

Several locations, including:
Scottish Poetry Library, 5 Crichton's Close, Canongate, Edinburgh EH8 8DT
Scottish Storytelling Centre, 43–45 High Street, Edinburgh EH1 1SR
National Library of Scotland, George IV Bridge, Edinburgh EH1 1EW
Central Library, 7–9 George IV Bridge, Edinburgh EH1 1EG
National Museum of Scotland Research Library, Chambers Street, Edinburgh EH1 1JF
Blackwells Bookshop 53-59 South Bridge, Edinburgh EH1 1YS
Filmhouse, 88 Lothian Road, Edinburgh EH3 9BZ
• www.scottishpoetrylibrary.org.uk/library/exhibitions/gifted-edinburgh-book-sculptures

A bookish Banksy

I n March 2011 a librarian at the Scottish Poetry Library found a small box left on a table. It contained a miniature tree, sculpted out of the leaves of a book: not origami but layers of thin printed paper discs, glued together to form a solid trunk, branching out into intricate papery foliage. At its base, resting on a thick hardback novel, was a gold-leaf-lined paper eggshell, hatching the words of "A Trace of Wings" by Edwin Morgan. His collection is housed at the Poetry Library. In tiny letters on a tag was the library's twitter handle, a truncated Patrick Geddes quote: @byleaveswelive. A short accompanying note explained that this was the inspiration for the piece. "This is for you," it said, "in support of libraries, books, words, ideas … a gesture (poetic maybe?)."

Then in June another sculpture turned up at the National Library of Scotland: a paper gramophone with a coffin rolling into the pages below it. The sculpted book was Ian Rankin's *Exit Music* in which his Edinburgh detective, Rebus, retires. Over the next few months, another eight sculptures, several with Rankin references, appeared at Edinburgh cultural institutions. Not all were strictly literary – the Filmhouse received a paper cinema with horses charging out of the screen towards the audience, one of whom was Rankin drinking his favourite pint, Deuchars IPA.

The eighth piece to be found was labelled the tenth in the series and is perhaps the most exquisite of them all. The artist had made the impossible things mentioned in Norman MacCaig's poem, "Gifts". You can see the delicate "gloves of bee's fur" and "cap of the wren's wings" behind glass in the basement of the Poetry Library; their minutely flocked surfaces must have been painstakingly carved using a razor blade and a magnifying glass.

But if this was the tenth, where were the other two? The hunt was on. And then suddenly the National Museum of Scotland found a tiny Tyrannosaurus Rex bursting out of the pages of Conan Doyle's *The Lost World*, and the Writers' Museum stumbled across an Edinburgh tenement street scene hidden in their Robert Louis Stevenson Room with a quote from *Jekyll and Hyde*.

The National Library has a display of five new pieces that were subsequently commissioned from the artist without ever meeting her. You have to see the pieces up close to understand quite how extraordinary they are. Start at the Poetry Library and follow the paper trail up the hill …

MUSEUM OF FIRE

76–78 Lauriston Place, Edinburgh EH3 9DE
• Tel: 0131 228 2401
• Open Mon–Fri 10am–3pm. Call before you visit to ensure a volunteer is free to attend
• Buses: 12, 27, 35, 45, 47

First brigade

The world's very first municipal fire service was established here in Edinburgh in 1824 by a 24-year-old local man – James Braidwood – who revolutionised fire fighting, wrote the first texts on the science of fire engineering and went on to become the director of the nascent London Fire Brigade. A statue of Braidwood stands behind St Giles' Cathedral, which his forces saved from the great fire of Edinburgh, a blaze which started only two months after he'd formed the city's fire brigade.

So it is a proud history that is traced in the museum at the eastern headquarters of the Scottish Fire and Rescue Service, just next to the Art College. It's so unadvertised that even the art students walk past and fail to notice the gleam of red fire engines, the glint of highly polished brass. The former fire station is crammed with beautifully restored early fire apparatus, including the first hand pump the brigade ever bought in 1824. It had no brakes so if the fire didn't get you, you might well be crushed by the runaway pump. It needed volunteers to pump the levers (hard work!), so they were encouraged by the offer of free beer while they toiled. The arrangement proved not to be conducive to sustained labour, so a token system was developed, allowing the volunteers to drink in all the pubs on their way home.

The museum is now run by (entirely sober) volunteer retired firefighters, who will not only supervise your visit but, if you chat to them, will also tell you amazing stories – tales of tragedy, horror and heroism, laced with gallows humour and moments of bizarre farce.

On display are historical artefacts and mementos from dramatic blazes, like a light bulb from the Empire Theatre where the Great Lafayette perished (see p. 233). Pinned to one wall is the sturdy but small jump sheet that Braidwood invented and an amazing action photo of a woman descending fast towards it, fifteen men holding it taut, bracing themselves for impact. On the opposite wall is what must be the world's largest collection of toy fire engines, all perfectly aligned and locked securely behind glass display cases, like a 5-year-old's torture fantasy. That might be the only downside of the museum: the engines are so appealing to children that it will take a stern dose of parenting to stop them clambering all over these lovingly preserved, antique machines.

EDINBURGH CAST COLLECTION

Main building, Edinburgh College of Art, 74 Lauriston Place, Edinburgh
EH3 9DF
• Tel: 0131 651 5800
• Email: eca.ed.ac.uk
• Open daily: 9am–5pm. Admission free: please report to reception on arrival
• Buses: 2, 23, 27, 35, 45, 47

> *Losing your marbles*

The Cast Collection at Edinburgh College of Art is one of the finest neoclassical ensembles in Europe. And yet the casts are usually out of sight when the public are invited in for degree shows or Sculpture Court parties. Even when the replicas are in situ, the students tend to brush past them, more focused on the modern, the abstract, the conceptual.

The Sculpture Court itself was designed to hang one of only two existing casts of the Parthenon marbles. They used the same measurements as the original Nike temple, and hung the casts at the same height and behind a colonnade, just as they were in Athens. The frieze depicts the Great Panathenaia, a four-yearly celebratory procession through the streets of Athens. The originals are controversially kept safe at the British Museum, having been "rescued" from the Parthenon by Lord Elgin in 1801. The casts that now hang in the ECA were taken in 1836, before the British Museum's curators somewhat roughly cleaned up the originals, using sandpaper, chisels and acid. So what you see in this replica is, bizarrely, more authentic than the originals.

There are other amazing casts in the collection. "Smugglerius", a disturbing 1776 anatomical sculpture of a man flayed alive for smuggling, the original of which has been lost. The headless antique marble, "Winged Victory of Samothrace", which once stood on a stone replica of a giant ship's prow. Upstairs in the north-east corridor is a dark bronze copy of Lorenzo Ghiberti's "Gates of Paradise", an exquisite pair of 15th-century bronze doors from the Baptistery of San Giovanni in Florence.

But most secret of all – so secret that you can't actually see them – are the casts that have been boarded up. If you could see through the plasterboard blocking the arches, you would find the tomb of Baron Ferry de Gros and his two wives, lying just as they do in St James's Church in Bruges. Princess Margaret from Lincluden Collegiate Church, one of the most elaborate monumental tombs surviving in Scotland. An altarpiece from the Church of the Ascension in the province of Siena. A fireplace from the Musée de Cluny in Paris. Over the last century, as modernism rose and the cult of the original took hold, the knowledge of the value this extraordinary collection has been gradually lost. But maybe one day soon, a brave prince or princess will battle their way through the plasterboard and awaken these sleeping beauties.

COVENANTERS' MEMORIAL ❹

87 Grassmarket, Edinburgh EH1 2LJ
• Open 24 hrs. Admission free
• Bus: 2

*Beneath
the shadow
of the gibbet*

On the ground at the Cowgate end of the Grassmarket is a raised stone disc with a glazed brick pattern in the shape of a martyr's cross. This discreet memorial commemorates over 100 Covenanters who were hanged between 1661 and 1688 for their refusal to accept the Stuart kings as head of the Presbyterian Church of Scotland.

The Covenanters were so called because they had signed the Covenant that protested at the royals interfering in their religion. They did not agree that the monarch had divine right and believed that only Jesus could be head of the Church. They were regarded as dangerous fundamentalists and could be executed on the spot if they refused to swear allegiance to the king. Many were hanged at the gibbet (gallows) right here. The other venue was up at the Mercat Cross on the Royal Mile.

Recently, the shadow of the gibbet has been marked on the paving, with names of the known Covenanters displayed on a plaque nearby.

NEARBY

COVENANTERS' PRISON
Greyfriars cemetery, Candlemaker Row, Edinburgh EH1 2QQ
Cemetery open daily during daylight hours
• Greyfriars Museum open April–Oct: Mon–Fri 10.30am–4.30pm, Sat 11am–2pm. Admission free

Greyfriars cemetery is only a 5-minute walk from the Grassmarket if you enter from the bottom via steps from Candlemaker Row. This is where the National Covenant was signed in 1637: one of the rare original copies is on display in the church's museum. Less than fifty years after their statement of defiance, the Covenanters were defeated by King Charles II at the battle of Bothwell Brig in 1679. One thousand, two hundred survivors were imprisoned in terrible conditions in a field inside the Telfer Wall, which is now a gated-off area of Greyfriars known as the Covenanters' Prison. With no roof to shelter them, and fed only a handful of bread a day, many died, some were executed, some escaped, and others were freed on signing allegiance to the king. The last 257 were sentenced to transportation to the American penal colonies. But the ship was wrecked in the Orkney islands and only 48 survived.

The executioner of most of the Covenanters was one George Mackenzie, the King's Advocate, who is also buried in Greyfriars – right next to the Covenanters' Prison. There are many tales of people developing strange wounds and grazes, apparently being swiped at by his blood-lusting poltergeist, earning him the nickname "Bloody" Mackenzie.

Watch out for another troubling element of the graveyard: the mortsafe, a 19th-century lockable iron cage that fitted over a grave to keep the contents safe from body-snatching grave robbers.

SCOTTISH GENEALOGY CENTRE

15 Victoria Terrace, Edinburgh EH1 2JL
- Tel: 0131 220 3677
- www.scotsgenealogy.com
- Email: enquiries@scotsgenealogy.com
- Open Mon, Tues, Thurs & Fri 10.30am–5.30pm, Wed 10.30am–7.30pm, Sat 10–5pm
- Membership: £20 per year
- Buses: 23, 27, 41, 42, 67

Special branch

To find the Scottish Genealogy Centre, you have to be determined. You must take the narrow terrace which runs above Victoria Bow and follow it past the main shops, through the black iron gate and on round the corner to almost the end, where you will eventually come to a bright blue door.

But if you are interested in tracing your family tree, this is only the first hurdle. What you are about to undertake is pretty much full-blown detective work, riddled with red herrings, tampered evidence, unreliable witnesses and dead-end alleys. It looks easy on the TV shows, but they cut out all the detail: to track down your culprits, you will need to search painstakingly through paperwork, decipher scrawled handwriting and cross-reference microfilm with parish records, telephone directories, scrolled maps and crumbling headstones.

But should you wish to take on such a detail, the volunteer staff and facilities at the Scottish Genealogy Centre will make the process a whole lot easier … and markedly cheaper. Ancestry is big business – there are numerous websites out there, monetising their track-and-trace assistance. You can rack up quite a bill chasing an elusive relative. But the SGC have subscriptions to the main sites and you can do unlimited searches from their computers: their membership is your membership. Also included in your annual fee is access to their reference library, which is equipped for every police procedural: its vaulted walls are lined with sections on military records, pre-1841 censuses, kirk sessions, tax records, monumental inscriptions, and birth, marriage and death records.

There's another intriguing detail in this case. The vast job of transferring all the records onto microfilm was paid for and undertaken by the Mormons. Yes, the Mormons from Utah. Because as part of their faith, they want to track down their ancestors so they can vicariously baptise them. Somewhere up in the Utah hills are huge vaults containing 2.5 million rolls of microfilmed genealogical records from all over the world.

But if it's the Scottish branches of your tree under investigation, you'll have plenty to work with here. You're likely to bump into people who have spent half their lives tracking down their clan, happy to exhaust entire weekends at these desks, obsessively rifling records. Now that's good police.

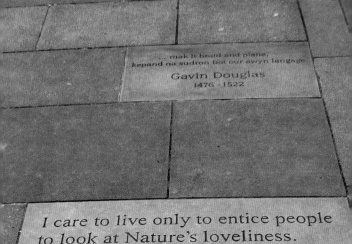

... mak it braid and plane,
kepand na sudron bot our awyn langage

Gavin Douglas
1476 - 1522

I care to live only to entice people
to look at Nature's loveliness.

John Muir   1838 - 1914

gh tyrants threat, though Lyons rage and
Defy them all, and feare not to win out

Elizabeth Melville,
Lady Culross, c.1578 - c.1640

MAKARS' COURT

6

Lady Stair's Close, Lawnmarket, Edinburgh EH1 2PA
• Open 24 hrs. Admission free
• Buses: 6, 23, 27, 41, 42, 67

*Poetic
paving stones*

As you near the top of the mound, there is a gap between Nos 9 and 11 North Bank Street, with four flights of steps leading up into Lady Stair's Close. The close can also be entered from the top of the Royal Mile at the second and third archways after Deacon Brodie's Tavern: the former, labelled "Lady Stair's", has the Writers' Museum sign hanging above it; and the latter, labelled "Gladstone's Land", has the golden eagle swooping overhead.

But instead of looking up, you should be looking down. Step slowly because you are walking on the most eloquent of paving. On an overcast day, you can easily miss it: the shallow markings in the grey stone need bright light to lift their contrast. Look carefully and you will see that the erudite words of Scotland's greatest poets, bards and writers (known as makars) are engraved on the flagstones, forming an evolving literary monument just outside the Writers' Museum.

Robert Louis Stevenson's declaration that "There are no stars so lovely as Edinburgh street-lamps" gets a slab. Elsewhere Neil M. Gunn's views on nuts and salmon are recorded. Another stone features a passage from Hugh MacDiarmid's "A Drunk Man Looks at the Thistle". The oldest lines here were written by John Barbour in 1375: "A! Fredome is a noble thing" is from "The Bruce", the earliest surviving poem written in Scots. The famous diarist James Boswell attributes his "I rattled down the High Street in high elevation of spirits!" to having walked nearby in 1762.

Elizabeth Melville's words from 1604 show that Scots women have never been faint of heart: "Though tyrants threat, though Lyons rage and rore, Defy them all, and feare not to win out." Naomi Mitchison points out: "Go back far enough and all humankind are cousins." George Buchanan, Scotland's greatest Latin poet, shows that democracy was alive in Scotland even in the mid-16th century: "*Populo enim jus est ut imperium cui velit deferat*" (For it is right that the people confer power on whom they please).

John Muir, East Lothian-born father of environmentalism and the man who persuaded Ted Roosevelt to preserve the wilderness that forms California's national parks, is commemorated by his words, "I care to live only to entice people to look at Nature's loveliness."

And the last line from Muriel Spark's *The Prime of Miss Jean Brodie*, also inscribed here, mentions "*The Transfiguration of the Commonplace* …" which could in fact be a description of this inspirational courtyard.

If you feel the urge to follow in the footsteps of many of Edinburgh finest writers, the award-winning edinburghliterarypubtour.co.uk will take you on a tipple-filled tour of their drinking haunts.

THE SCOTSMAN STEPS: *WORK NO. 1059*

Top entrance: next to the Scotsman Hotel, 32 North Bridge, Edinburgh EH1 1QG
Lower entrance: between the City Art Centre and the Scotsman Hotel, 1 Market Street, Edinburgh EH1 1DE
• Open from early to late. Free admission
• Buses: 5, 7, 8, 14, 35, 45, 39

International marble sampler

The Scotsman Steps are a permanent installation by the artist Martin Creed, opened in 2011 and commissioned by the Fruitmarket Gallery and Edinburgh World Heritage for the festival. Creed is most famous for his Turner Prize-winning *Work No. 227: The lights going on and off*, which was pretty much self-explanatory. Conceived ten years later, *Work No. 1059* continues his interest in progress and movement, forcing the viewer to step through the space to appreciate it. Edinburgh struck Creed as being full of staircases, this being one of the longest. He wrote a rather whiney song about it: "Staircase. In nearly every case there's a staircase. And then ... there's another staircase. And then another ... staircase."

This one used to be a bit of a dodgy descent, mainly used as a homeless shelter or a gigantic urinal by passers-by. So it was entirely appropriate that Creed remade the steps in hygienic marble. But this is far more extravagant than your average Armitage Shanks. Each of the 104 steps is clad in a different marble, sourced from all around the world and each with its unique colour, swirls and mottlings.

White marble is very pure limestone which has been compressed and heated until it metamorphoses into a crystalline structure, with patterns and colours caused by impurities like clay, sand or metals. One of the steps has embedded fossils beneath its polished surface. Many samples are from Italy, like Bianco Gioia, Arabescato Carrara and Grey Saint Laurent – Creed himself lives just north of Sicily on the island of Alicudi. But there are others from further afield: pale cream Bianco Namibia from south-west Africa, dark pink Rosa Portogallo from Portugal, heavy yellow Sunset Gold from Lebanon ...

The steps connect the Old Town and the New, down the side of what used to be the offices of *The Scotsman*. There were once windows into the stairwell, so pedestrians could buy their paper direct and read it as they trudged onwards. The Art College used to run a competition with *The Scotsman* and the winning works were displayed on the steps. Now the steps are a work of art in themselves: they are protected by wrought-iron gates which are locked every night after the last train and opened in the morning with the arrival of the first.

ST GILES' CATHEDRAL ROOFTOP

- Email: stgilestower@gmail.com
- Open May–Sept: Mon–Fri 10am–7pm, Sat 10am–5pm, Sun 1pm–5pm. Oct–April: Mon–Sat 10am–5pm, Sun 1pm–5pm
- Admission £6
- Buses: 35, 23, 27, 28, 41, 42

Striking distance

St Giles' holds many a secret in its ancient walls, as there has been a church on this site since the year 854. But it is only very recently that we have been allowed up to explore the roof. The twenty-minute rooftop tour allows only four people at a time, so it's best to book your place in advance, though you could always turn up on the slim chance that it's not quite full.

The guide will take you up the 91 winding steps which emerge out onto the lead roof 20 metres above the High Street. There is a narrow gangway leading up to the bell tower, where you can stop and admire the view. Up towards the Observatory and the Castle, and down towards Holyrood and Portobello, this is a section of the Royal Mile that you don't normally see as it is always blocked by, well, St Giles'. Below are the grotesques – the term for non-operational gargoyles – their dry-mouthed, angry stone faces jutting out from the roof edge. You can get up close and personal with one which is right above the doorway from the stairwell – a lion-like face with wide cheeks and big eyes, reminiscent of a Chinese New Year dragon.

From the gangway you enter the little door into the bell tower itself. The internal timber frame looks just like the final scenes of Hitchcock's *Vertigo*, though thankfully with no stairs to climb. There used to be thirty-five musical bells in here but now there are just three, which chime every quarter hour –

so you are likely to be within striking distance. The green and gold 1912 clock mechanism is preserved in a glass case, and you can watch it whirring round like something which has escaped from the Chambers Street Museum. The guide will usually show you the precious remnants of the clock faces, which used to front the tower, and the old weather cock which topped it back in 1567.

As you re-enter the stairwell, notice the graffiti left by successive stone masons. And be careful on your descent: the camber is not so friendly going down!

See overleaf for another secret hidden in St Giles' Cathedral.

THE TEMPLARS AND THE THISTLE

The current Order of the Thistle was created in 1687 by King James VII of Scotland, but it dates back to the Middle Ages. Some historians say that the Knights of the Thistle are actually a branch of the Order of the Knights Templar. So dashing in their red-crossed white tunics, the Templar knights were essentially the SAS of medieval mounted soldiers. While half of them fought in the Crusades, the others ran a kind of early European banking system. But unfortunately, the battle for the Holy land was lost and so was their popularity. King Philip IV of France owed them a lot of money and decided that rather than repay it, he would have them all tortured and burned at the stake.

In 1312, when the Pope acquiesced to Philip's demands and disbanded the Order, there were suddenly no Templar knights to be seen anywhere. But then, strangely, some very Templar-esque knights popped up in Scotland and enlisted to fight for Robert the Bruce in the battle against the English. Rumour has it that they were pivotal in the Scots victory at Bannockburn in 1314. However, since one of their rules was "no fighting other Christians", they mainly helped behind the scenes. As a reward, King Robert allowed them to form the Order of the Thistle in 1334, with an almost identical set-up to the Knights Templar. The next year he allowed them to merge with the Order of the Eastern Knights, another branch of the KTs. Some say that these Eastern Knights were the origins of the Freemasonic "Order of Heredom", which is why Scottish Freemasonry attributes its origins to the foundation of the Order of the Thistle.

If you want to see the modern Order of the Thistle, visit the Thistle Chapel, a small but highly ornate room in the back of St Giles. It isn't always open, and to see it you must be escorted by one of the stewards. The chapel is dedicated to the Order of the Thistle: sixteen Scots who have been knighted by the monarch in recognition of their outstanding service. The vaulted ceiling is covered with the most complex cat's cradle pattern you've ever seen, while the walls are lined with beautifully carved stalls, one for each of the knights and ladies and two for the royals. Atop each stall is the crest of the current knight, while those of his predecessors line the back. Any knight who has the misfortune to lack a family crest is allowed to invent one. So there are leaping jaguars, Earth globes with rainbows, and a green monster with red toenails who might well be related to Godzilla. Not quite the stuff of the medieval chivalric code, but even secret orders need to update sometimes.

JOHN
BLAW
Smith left to
the Poor of
this Chapell £20 St
Died at Canton in
CHINA 18 Aug 1729

I.
Copp
Son of
the Po
House
he Die
Ag

THOMAS
LAUDER SONE to
ABOVE IOHN LAUDER
COPERSMITH LEFt to
THIS HOUSE 100 MERK
S WAS PAYED BE IEAN
CAMPBEL HIS MOTHER
HE DYED 15 IAN'R 1731
AGED 21 YEARS

MAGDALEN CHAPEL

41 Cowgate, Edinburgh EH1 1JR
• Open Tues, Thurs & Fri 10am–2pm
• Otherwise by appointment with Rev. Sinclair. Home tel: 0131 621 1599
Or via the Scottish Reformation Society:
info@scottishreformationsociety.org
• Bus: 2

Home of the Hammermen

The Magdalen Chapel is a tiny wee place hidden at the end of the Cowgate just before it opens up into the Grassmarket. It seems to cower under the towering arch of the George IV Bridge, though it was built nearly three hundred years earlier in 1541. Inside is Scotland's only remaining medieval stained glass, with four modest but beautiful roundels depicting coats of arms: Mary of Guise's, the Lion Rampant of Scotland, and those of Michael MacQuhane and his wife Janet Rynd.

MacQuhane, a wealthy moneylender, commissioned the chapel as he was dying because he "esteemed it ane good Way to obtain Eternal Life".

The main chapel was also to be used by the Hammermen – a sort of trades union for Edinburgh craftsfolk who worked "with hammer and with hand", i.e. blacksmiths, armourers, buckle-makers, but also saddlers, clockmakers and (rather worryingly) surgeons. A stone carving of a Hammerman in his traditional dress hangs by the window and you can see their crests painted on the curved wooden screen which embraces the hall. All around the walls are "brods" – dark wooden panels inscribed with gold letters, each detailing and dating a Hammerman and his donation. Essentially a highly decorative form of bookkeeping.

Beneath the window is a small dark table, now covered with leaflets and postcards, but upon which once rested the headless bodies of executed Scottish Covenanters. Helen Alexander, heroine of the Covenanters, who went to prison several times for giving them hospitality, managed to win the right for those executed to receive a Christian burial instead of being dumped in mass graves. And so their bodies were brought here before being buried in Greyfriars.

Standing proud at the head of the chapel is the ornate deacon's chair, originally crafted in 1708 and remade in 2000. Thanks to the Hammermen's obsession with financial documentation, the restorers were able to find each item used in its making, including "200 takets" and "Russian Leather for do.", totalling £2.50. Amazingly they managed to procure some Russian leather from exactly that period, salvaged intact from the wreck of the *Metta Catharina*, which went down in 1786 off the coast of Cornwall. The cost of the renovation? £7,000. Duly noted.

> It is thought that the first General Assembly of the Church of Scotland was held here in 1560, presided over by John Knox himself.

ANDY GOLDSWORTHY'S "HUTTON ROOF"

National Museum of Scotland, Chambers Street, Edinburgh EH1 1JF
• Tel: 0300 123 6789
• www.nms.ac.uk/national-museum-of-scotland
• Open daily 10am–5pm. Roof terrace closed if icy/dangerous weather
• Buses: 2, 23, 27, 35, 41, 42, 45, 67, CS1

Sculptural oversight

Everyone knows the National Museum of Scotland on Chambers Street, but few visitors manage to find the rooftop garden. No, I don't mean the Tower Restaurant, with its terrace overlooking Chambers Street and Greyfriars. I mean two floors up from that: the beautiful decked platform with a 360° view around the city and the wonderful Andy Goldsworthy sculptures. Not been? Then choose a clear day and get up there: it's a wonderful place.

There is a lift directly up to the seventh level from the Terrace Lift, which is in the "Kingdom of the Scots" gallery near the tower entrance. But as the lifts often break down, you might have to take the "scenic lift" behind the racing car up to the fifth floor and then climb the spiral staircase. Assuming it's not treacherously icy or blowing a gale, you will be allowed up. You emerge onto a grey striped wooden deck with white walls, plants all around the edges and four large lumps of rock in the middle. Don't eschew them in favour of the view: these are Andy Goldsworthy's "Hutton Roof" sculptures. "Hutton" as in the Edinburgh geologist James Hutton (see p. 47), who first worked out that you could track the Earth's history by examining the erosion of rocks.

Goldsworthy, who always works with natural materials, took four blocks of pinky orange sandstone from a quarry near his Dumfriesshire home. The sandstone is compacted from the sands of a 270 million-year-old desert. He split the blocks along their grain, carved decreasing sized holes into each layer and then reconstructed the blocks. The result is what looks like a layered rock hole through which you can peer down into what Hutton called "deep time". Or you could throw litter into it, presumably thinking it's a rather ornate bin. (Pay attention, kids!)

The planting round the edges of the roof is organised to replicate the plants natural to the landscape you can view beyond them. So as you look north towards the sea, you will be next to coastal vegetation. And as you look south towards Blackford Hill, you will find mountain plants at your fingertips. It's hard to concentrate on the plants, though, as the views are so spectacular – across to Fife, down to the mountains and over all the other rooftops of this inspiring city.

PARLIAMENT HALL

11 Parliament Square, Edinburgh EH1 1RF
- Tel: 0131 225 2595
- Email: kglen@scotcourt.gov.uk
- Open Mon–Fri 10am–4pm. Admission free
- Buses: 2, 23, 27, 41, 42, 45

The last Parliament

Edinburgh's residents know they can visit the Scottish Parliament building, which opened in 2004. But far fewer of them realise that, a ten minutes' stroll up the Royal Mile, they can walk into the debating hall where the last Parliament of Scotland sat some three hundred years ago, before the controversial Act of Union.

Parliament Hall is just across the car park behind St Giles' Cathedral, and is open to the public, but doesn't really advertise itself. Though it was built as a permanent home for the Scottish Parliament, after the union with England in 1707 it was looked after by the Faculty of Advocates and soon became the home of the Supreme Court. It looks as if it's closed to visitors, but if you ask permission at reception, they will let you wander through into this extraordinary historic debating chamber.

High above you is a hammer-beam roof – a self-supporting, nail-free wooden engineering feat, just as impressive as that marvelled at down in Westminster. The slap of polished legal sole on varnished wooden floorboard echoes around the vast space, as the advocates march importantly up and down, taking calls on their mobiles. The size of the hall allows them the audio equivalent of being hidden in plain sight – avoiding confidential conversations being overheard by keeping on the move. The walls are stuffed with portraits (many by Henry Raeburn) of Edinburgh's parliamentary and legal grandees – including Henry Erskine, the politician and lawyer who in 1788 was given the job of defending Deacon Brodie, on trial in this very hall. A task at which, it must be said, Erskine was not entirely successful. Look carefully and you will see the wee window high up in the wall where a man, standing on a very tall ladder, used to poke his head through to call the court to session.

You'd think a structure this size would be hard to misplace, but strange to tell, Edinburgh City Council seems to have accidentally "lost" Parliament Hall. In 2006, when thousands of pounds were about to be spent on refurbishing it, the Scottish Government checked that the City owned the property, and someone in the council mistakenly said no. So the names of the Faculty of Advocates and the Scottish Court Services were duly entered on the title deeds. Oops! A lengthy debate is sure to ensue …

BLAIR STREET VAULTS

28 Blair Street, Edinburgh EH1 1QR
• Access only with Mercat Tours: www.mercattours.com
• Buses: 5, 7, 8, 14, 45, 49

*Safe from
the Securitate*

Now that Mary King's Close has become an international tourist attraction, those of us who like to burrow have to delve further down to explore Edinburgh's secret underworld. Just below the Tron bar on Blair Street is an inauspicious opening into an underground world of cavernous vaults between the supporting structures of the South Bridge – the long, hidden bridge which carries the A7 from the High Street, over the valley that is the Cowgate, onto Chambers Street. Built in 1788, it was to link the centre to the Southside and the university area.

To support the bridge, layers of archways were constructed – nineteen arches spanning some 300 metres. The gaps between the arches looked rather useful, so floors were built to create rooms that were used as storage or rented out as artisans' workshops. Soon there was a thriving underground craftsworld of cobblers, milliners, smelters and the like. There were even oyster bars with an edgy atmosphere that made them terribly fashionable for well-heeled folk who wanted to kick off said footwear.

But being a dark and hidden space, it also attracted people who didn't want to be seen. Meetings of the Hellfire Club were held here for "persons of quality" who wished to take part in immoral acts. Soon Burke and Hare were hiding their bodies down there, and there was even a convenient body-sized passageway leading up the university medical department (see p. 140). The place became so dangerous that only thirty years after opening, the council decided to brick it up, using rubble gathered from the city's many fires.

Over a hundred and fifty years later, in the early 1980s, ex-rugby international Norrie Rowan, who owned the Tron bar, discovered a passageway leading into the vaults from his pub and started, rather unofficially, to clear the space. Soon Edinburgh bands were renting the rooms for rehearsals. Fringe performances and night clubs were held there. At one point it even served as a hiding place for the Romanian rugby player Cristian Raducanu, aided by Rowan in his escape from the Romanian secret police just before the 1989 uprising. Recently things got a bit more official and archaeologists and historians became involved. Now you can only visit the vaults with Mercat Tours, either as part of their "Historic Underground" tour or, if you'd prefer a more gothic experience, through one of their ghost tours and vigils.

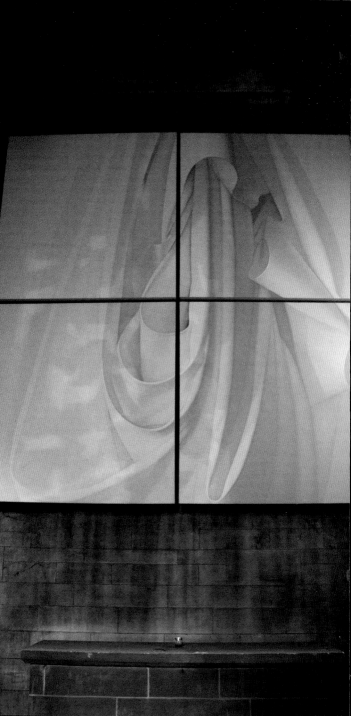

STILL BY ALISON WATT

Chapel of Old St Paul's Church
63 Jeffrey Street, Edinburgh EH1 1DH
• Open 8am– 6pm
• Admission free
• Behind Waverley Station
• Buses: 6, 41, 42

> *The fabric of loss*

Old St Paul's Church is a bit of a hidden gem: its narrow façade, hemmed in on the lower slope of Jeffrey Street, hardly hints at the TARDIS-like space inside. The present church was built in 1883, on the site of Scotland's first Episcopalian church, where people have worshipped since 1689. Take the thirty-three wide Calvary steps up to the first floor and you will find a vast secluded nave, which has been extended three times. Above is a hammer-beam roof with wooden gargoyles to guard the top of each column.

In the corner nearest the stairs is a memorial chapel. It was built to honour the lives lost in the First and Second World Wars. And it is in this chapel that you will find Greenock-born artist Alison Watt's huge painting, *Still*, installed in 2004 as part of the International Festival.

Still is 12 feet high and spans across four 6-foot canvas panels, a simple and yet abstract image of hanging folds of fabric, painted in soft whites and greys. The panels are suspended above head height and seem to glow, despite being only dimly lit by the natural light from the adjacent window. The dark gaps between them form a cross. The drapes of material seem to suggest the ghostly traces of someone who is now absent. The piece echoes with the history of fabric in religious paintings and stories – the folds of the Virgin Mary's headdress, the Turin Shroud, St Veronica's veil …

Watt wanted to create an image which conveyed the emotion she felt upon entering the chapel: an overwhelming sadness. Her early work focused on female nudes and then started to depict them with draped material, inspired by the paintings of Ingres. Soon she was entirely focused on the fabric itself – the imprint left on sheets by the body, and then abstracted to just the details of the folds themselves.

In many ways, *Still* is Watt's most successful painting; looser and freer than many of her other works, its scale and location force the viewer to step back and admire it as a whole.

Watt's studio is down in Drummond Place and if you spot her, you'll be surprised at how small and dainty the creator of this vast piece is.

In 2008 Watt was invited to be the seventh (and youngest) artist in residence at the National Gallery, London, which was where as a child she had seen Ingres' portrait of Madame Moitessier, draped in the finery of her flower-patterned dress.

GEDDES MEMORIAL

Trunks Close, 55 High Street, Edinburgh EH1 1SR
• www.cockburnassociation.org.uk
• Open 24 hrs
• Admission free
• Buses: 6, 35

Beehiving himself

Trunks Close is a very narrow gunnel behind the steps up to Moubray House, one of the oldest on the High Street. Sadly, the house itself is currently closed to the public – although it contains an amazing Renaissance ceiling and wall paintings. But down the side, you can see the basement of the building, which is the home of the Cockburn Association, the Edinburgh Civic Trust that organises the Doors Open Day each year in late September and so is a fount of knowledge for all things architectural. The association is named after Lord Henry Cockburn (1779–1854), who campaigned to protect and enhance the beauty of Edinburgh.

If you keep walking down past the Cockburn Association, you'll find an opening into a tiny hidden garden, belonging to Sandeman House where the Scottish Book Trust is based. It's almost always empty and so an ideal place to find the peace and quiet to read a book – you might even find one lying there for you to borrow or swap. At the far edge of the circular lawn is a large bronze cockerel (the Cockburn Association's insignia) and, at the near edge, a statue of the extraordinary polymath and father of environmental town planning, Patrick Geddes. This is one of his keyhole gardens which allowed light and space into an overcrowded Old Town. The sculpture is by Kenny Hunter, who is head of sculpture at Edinburgh College of Art. He has placed Geddes on a beehive-shaped plinth.

"Geddes studied and wrote widely on bees and would have appreciated more than most their vital role on this planet," says Hunter. "I gravitated toward the expressive potential of the beehive both as a functioning plinth and metaphor. The beehive evokes his life, work and the dissemination of his ideas."

PATRICK GEDDES

Patrick Geddes (1854–1932) was one of the most internationally influential philosophers of urban planning. The son of a Ballater soldier, he studied biology, sociology and geography, was recognised by the Royal Society at 25 and counted Charles Darwin, Mahatma Gandhi and Albert Einstein among his admirers. In his mission to solve the slum housing and sanitation problems of Edinburgh's Old Town, Geddes moved from his affluent house in the New Town to James Court at the top of the Royal Mile. He believed that to understand a community, you had to live there. He insisted that instead of flattening sites and rebuilding them from scratch along the inorganic perpendicular gridiron lines of the New Town, it was better to observe how people use a space and then gently, surgically intervene to organically adapt the existing architecture. His work can be spotted all around the Old Town, where he conserved buildings, allowed traffic to flow and transformed disused or derelict spaces into gardens to allow some light and breathing space into the urban density. Geddes wrote: "The world is mainly a vast leaf colony, growing on and forming a leafy soil, not a mere mineral mass: and we live not by the jingling of our coins, but by the fullness of our harvests."

You can see other Geddes gardens at 1 Mound Place, 5 Johnston Terrace and Granny's Green off the Grassmarket, where his daughter also designed the Westport Garden.

JAMES HUTTON MEMORIAL GARDEN

3 St John's Hill (enter from 46 Pleasance)
• www.edinburghgeolsoc.org
• Open 24 hours
• Buses: 6, 60

Rock garden

You can't miss the huge white dome that is "Our Dynamic Earth", built as a tribute to James Hutton, the Edinburgh-born father of geology. But his Memorial Garden is much harder to find. You can reach it from Viewcraig Gardens by climbing the steps which you'll find on the first bend up from Holyrood Road. But the simplest route is probably to go through the car park at the side of the University Sports Centre at 46 Pleasance, right opposite the foot of Drummond Street. Walk under the archway, to the back of the car park, and on your left you should spot the entrance to the path down to the garden, between parking bays 20 and 21.

Halfway between these two levels, you'll find a small loose gravel circle containing six seemingly inauspicious stones. These stones are actually the basis of modern geology, Darwinism and even Gaia theory. It was observing stones like these that led Hutton to work out his Plutonism theory: that the granite was molten rock spewed out by volcanoes and then worn away, rejecting the previous Neptunism theory which held that all rocks were thrown up by the sea. And Hutton calculated that the Earth had to be millions of years old, formed by the same mechanisms which were still at play, thereby laying the foundation for Darwin's theory of evolution.

This garden marks the spot where James Hutton lived from the age of 42 right up until his death aged 71 in 1797. The man was no stationary stone-spotter; he was quite the traveller, drinker and womaniser. He wrote to his friend, the steam engine inventor James Watt, suggesting it would be an even better idea to build a steam-powered sex machine.

Living here, Hutton would have gazed daily out of his window onto the ancient volcano that is Arthur's Seat. At the east end of the Salisbury Crags is an area of geological pilgrimage known as "Hutton's Section": seams of igneous dolerite are twisted up through sedimentary sandstone. (If you want to find it, download the "Rock Opera" app by Hoda Productions which will take you on a playful and informative guided tour.) And if you stand on the very top of Arthur's Seat, on a clear day you might see as far down the coast as Siccar Point near Cockburnspath, where you can visit one of the amazing rock formations known as Hutton's Unconformity. Well worth a trip – and it's barely a stone's throw away.

EDINBURGH MOSAIC

Paterson's Land, Old Moray House, Holyrood Road, Edinburgh EH8 8AQ
- Open Mon–Thurs 8.30am–5pm, Fri 8.30am–4.45pm
- Admission free, but ask permission to enter at reception
- Buses: 6, 60

A secret signing

The strange thing about Moray House teaching college is that the various buildings comprising the Holyrood Campus are called "lands" – Chessel's Land, Charteris Land, Dalhousie Land, St Leonard's Land, etc. Turns out it's a sixteenth-century term for a tenement building. In *Memorials of Edinburgh in the Olden Time* (1840s), Daniel Wilson describes a land as "a building of several stories of separate dwellings communicating by a common stair".

In Paterson's Land (built in 1911), on the wall above a doorway half-way up the main stairwell, you'll find a 60-square-foot (5.5 sq. m) panel of small square ceramic tiles called the Edinburgh Mosaic. It was created in 1938 by an Edinburgh School of Art student, William J. Macaulay, who had studied mosaics in Greece, Turkey and Palestine. His coloured-glass tiles are a distilled depiction of 1707 Edinburgh, steeply clustered with the Salisbury Crags on one side, the castle on the other, and nestling between them, Moray House itself. At the bottom is the blue sea of the Firth.

The Latin inscription around the border translates as: "In the garden of Moray House on 1 May 1707 the ambassadors of Scotland subscribed the Act of Union between Scotland and England."

It seems strange that such a beautiful and pastoral image represents what was at the time a hugely dramatic and violent upheaval. The garden to which the inscription refers is actually a car park round the side of Paterson's Land, the next entrance along Holyrood Road below. A small unobtrusive outhouse which backs on to the new student accommodation at Sugarhouse Close is what is referred to as the Summerhouse, and was once part of the beautiful gardens of Old Moray House.

In 1707 its tenant was the Earl of Seafield, Lord Chancellor of Scotland, whose job was to secure the controversial deal with England. Though the Union was supported by the Scottish aristocracy and ruling classes, it was vehemently opposed by the majority of Scots, who made their objections known by campaigning and rioting on the streets (scenes easily imagined by anyone who was in Scotland in 2014). The pavilion at the bottom of the Earl of Seafield's garden was perfect as a central and discreet location for Union supporters to meet, without attracting too much attention. While outside what was called the "Edinburgh Mob" rioted on the streets, the treaty was signed and rushed down to Westminster with a military escort. And so began the United Kingdom …

Behind the obelisk-pillared gates at the Canongate front is Old Moray House, built in 1618 for Mary, Countess of Home – the oldest building in the University of Edinburgh. You can see the countess's initials M and H above the centre window on the south wall. Inside, in the Cromwell and Balcony Rooms on the first floor, are some very fine and rare examples of seventeenth-century decorative plaster ceilings.

MONUMENTS COURTYARD COLLECTION

142–146 Canongate, Edinburgh EH8 8DD
Entry via Bakehouse Close or through the Museum of Edinburgh
• Museum open: Mon–Sat 10am–5pm. And Sun 12pm–5pm in August
• Bus: 35

*A home
for old stones*

Down the side of the Museum of Edinburgh is an archway into Bakehouse Close. As you walk through, there is a gateway on your right. If you're lucky it will be open and you can wander into a hidden flagstone courtyard which has become a kind of orphanage for historic stones without a home. Here all kinds of broken stones are welcomed, cleaned up and cherished: cracked monuments, dismembered statues, discarded sundials, pieced-together benches and fallen tombstones, all rescued from the rubble of the city and given a place to rest and recuperate in their old age.

The stones are arranged around the walled garden in slightly random but pleasing order, grouped thematically, among them flower beds and planters to bring some brighter colour to the monochrome hues. Along the back wall are Craft Incorporation stones from the 1600s – panels carved with the symbols and mottos of different artisan groups. A giant pair of scissors is the crest of Tailors Hall, which once stood in the Cowgate. The shoemakers have chosen a crown above a cordiner's (cobbler's) knife. On another stone, two men carry a barrel suspended between them on a pole – they are the "stingmen", or wine porters, who made drink deliveries from the port of Leith, their name deriving from *stang*, the old word for a wooden pole.

On the wall above a window is a stone carving of three charming maidens' faces which once topped a dormer window in the Old Town. Below is the far less pleasing countenance of a strangled man with his tongue lolling out, which was once part of a house in Dean Village. He might well agree with the inscription on the sundial from Saughton Gardens (see p. 197) which stands in the centre of the courtyard and roughly translates as "Take heed of time before time is taken from you."

Near the entrance archway are three innocent-looking stones which once formed part of the Netherbow Port, the gate into the city which, in the mid-1500s, stood just up the hill at the junction of the High Street and St Mary's Street. One of these stones is thought to be the site of the metal spike upon which countless criminal heads and other body parts were skewered and displayed as a warning to those considering a similar career trajectory.

The museum has created an interactive digital "window on the past" in the room adjoining the courtyard. It maps and details the different stones and also shows how the courtyard used to look in 1648 and 1884.

DUNBAR'S CLOSE

137 Canongate, High Street, Edinburgh EH8 8BW
• Open daily, dawn till dusk. Admission free
• Bus: 35

The Mushroom Garden

There are so many wee closes off the Royal Mile, it's easy to lose track of what leads where. Most gunnels take you down steep steps or into a crooked courtyard where some dreadful fire occurred or some stolen body was stored, or someone definitely did something nefarious at some point. But when you turn into Dunbar's Close (named after the writer David Dunbar, who back in 1773 owned tenements on either side), you emerge from the tunnel into an altogether more refined atmosphere. An elegant miniature 17th-century garden has been planted here, with lines of soft grey cobble or gravel paths edged by squares of low green box hedges. These segment the space into perfectly symmetrical beds containing lavender, tulip trees, morello cherries and espaliered apples. The feeling is of unexpected calm and order, as if you've entered a Jane Austen novel when you were expecting an episode of *True Detective*.

The garden is often referred to as the Mushroom Garden, which rather disappoints fungal foragers. The name actually derives from the fact that the Mushroom Trust, a Scottish charity that supports urban green spaces, saved the land from becoming an extension to the Scotsman car park. The trust bought the land and gifted it to the City of Edinburgh Parks Department, who had it redesigned by landscape architect Seamus Filor.

Filor chose a 17th-century design because that was when the gardens, which ran fishbone fashion from the central spine of the High Street, would have been at their most grand. Originally, the period planting was matched with elegant 17th-century-styled bins, until the local intelligentsia started using them as toilets. A flight of steps was built leading down to Calton Road, with a plan that it could lead across to Calton Hill. However, the developers on the next level refused permission, which is why you will find a holly bush cunningly disguising the cul-de-sac stairway.

There is a myth, commonly repeated on the internet and even by the council themselves, that the space was one of Patrick Geddes' gardens. However, research commissioned by the Mushroom Trust has established that there were tenements on the site until well after Geddes' death. Filor's perpendicular lines are rather in opposition to Geddes' anti-gridiron philosophy, but Geddes would certainly have approved of Dunbar's Close as it genuinely creates a green and tranquil breathing space within the hubbub of the working city.

Western Isles

THE STONES OF SCOTLAND

East end of Regents Road Park, Regent Road, Edinburgh [approximate postcode EH8 8EJ]
Three gates up from Regent Community Bowling Club
• Open 24 hrs
• Admission free
• Buses: 15, 104, 113

*A step
for Scotland
carved in stone*

The park running along the south side of Regents Park Road is often blocked from view by the barrier wall of tour buses. But not only is there a very pleasant stroll with spectacular views behind them, there is also a rather special art installation by the late George Wyllie MBE, who collaborated with artists Kenny Munro and Lesley-May Miller to gather stones from each of the thirty-two regions of Scotland. Wyllie's vision was to assemble the stones in a circle, with a steel ring encircling them and the footprint and the lone Scots pine at the centre.

The piece was opened in 2002 for the second anniversary of the Scottish Parliament, which you can see in the valley below. Wyllie said, "This work is a reminder to a new era of Scottish politics that the centre must involve and be legitimised by all that surrounds it." The stone plinth in the centre is indented by a footprint and a quote, "whose the tread that fits the mark", from a poem by Tessa Ransford, founder of the Scottish Poetry Library. The idea is that you place your foot in the footprint and then shout at the Scottish Parliament, which should hear the voices of Scots from all thirty-two council areas.

You might well guess that Aberdeen is represented by grey granite. From Stirling there's a lump of metamorphic rock collected from Tyndrum, where gold has been found on several occasions. You can see *stigmaria* – fossilised tree root on the lump of white sandstone from Midlothian. A chunk of Creetown Granite, also used to build the pillars of the George IV Bridge, represents Dumfries & Galloway. The oldest rock in the circle comes from the Western Isles – a 2,700 million-year-old lump of pink and grey boulder found on the seashore in Lewis.

Wyllie, Munro and Miller worked with landscape architect Stuart Rogers of the Paul Hogarth Company, who said the project was really enjoyable. Wyllie was particularly keen to find a skew-whiff tree for the centre: he wanted it to look as if it had grown in the wilderness, and not been farmed for logging. The artists had to persuade the Park Department not to keep the piece too over-manicured as Wyllie wanted it to look very natural – so the grass that has grown up between the stones is entirely part of the plan.

"A step for Scotland carved in stone, a parliament without a throne, a country each of us can own, a wisdom, knowing as we are known, a going forth and coming home. Who among us now will work, for light that penetrates the dark, for freedom climbing like the lark, for the democratic spark – whose the tread that fits this mark?" (Extract from *Incantation* by Tessa Ransford)

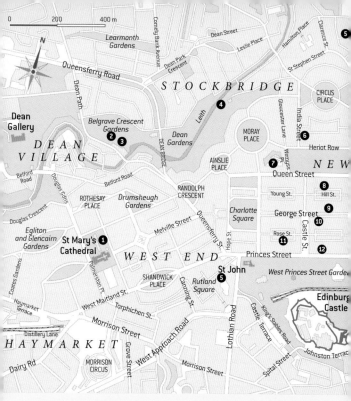

NEW TOWN

SONG SCHOOL

St Mary's Cathedral, Palmerston Place, Edinburgh EH12 5AW
- Tel: 0131 225 6293
- Email: office@cathedral.net
- Buses: 3, 4, 12, 25, 26, 31, 33, 44. Tram stop: Haymarket

> *If walls could sing*

In the grounds behind the West End's towering St Mary's Cathedral is a little hall where the choir practises. It's not really open to the public except during the August festival, but if you ask nicely at the cathedral and drop a few coins into their donation box, they may let you pop your head inside the Song School, as long as one of the choirs isn't actually in mid-rehearsal.

If you've never seen Phoebe Anna Traquair's work, prepare yourself for a mural epiphany. If you have – probably at the Mansfield Traquair Centre at the bottom of Broughton Street – then this is a chance to get really close up with Traquair's brushwork, to be enveloped in her riot of jewel-like colours and vivid characters. The images illustrate the lyrics of the canticle *"Benedicite, omnia opera Domine"*, aka "A Song of Creation", the idea being to fill the walls with visible song. Which is exactly the effect – the walls seem to vibrate with joy. The main chorus translates as "O all ye Works of the Lord, bless ye the Lord: praise him, and magnify him for ever."

Biblical scenes are shown against a Scottish landscape – with Leaderfoot Viaduct in the Borders featuring on the East Wall. In among the procession of heavenly and biblical figures, you may spot, to the right of the door, many faces of the Enlightenment – Tennyson, Browning and Rossetti, Thomas Carlyle and James Watts. And to the right of the organ, Dante, Cardinal Newman and of course William Blake, whose figurative style and love of colour were a clear influence on Traquair. If you look carefully, opposite the entrance, you will find the face of the artist herself.

The Song School was built in 1885, six years after St Mary's opened, and has been continuously in use ever since. By 1993 it had become pretty grey and grubby, so with the help of a Historic Scotland grant, the building and paintings were restored. The result is spectacular. The colours sing louder than any choir could. It's almost narcotic. And when you leave, you'll still see the afterburn of the images ringing joyously in your eyes.

In the cathedral next door, the Ascension-themed stained-glass windows were designed by Sir Eduardo Paolozzi.

WELL COURT

Dean Village, Edinburgh EH4 3BE
• Viewable from outside 24 hrs
• www.ewht.org.uk/well-court-3

From piss poor to tanfastic

As Sir John R. Findlay, owner of *The Scotsman* newspaper, looked out of his high window in Drumsheugh Gardens, he was appalled by the state of the tenements in the Dean Valley below. The Water of Leith powered flour mills and sluiced the tanneries, but since Telford had built his impressive 1832 Dean Bridge, the area was no longer a thoroughfare. With the flour mills being put out of business by the supermills down in Leith, the area was going into a decline. The only surviving industry was Robert Legget & Sons, the tannery.

In 1886 JRF had Well Court built as model housing for the tannery workers. It was designed by Sydney Mitchell, who went on to design Ramsay Garden up by the Castle – you can see a similarity in their Arts and Crafts stylings. Built in red sandstone with steep turrets and red pantiles, Well Court is centred around a communal courtyard. All the two- and three-room flats are different, giving an idiosyncratic, individualistic feel rather than uniform accommodation boxes. A hall provided a place to socialise, church attendance was compulsory on Sundays, and a clock tower reminded the inhabitants to be home by 10pm on week nights – or they'd be locked out. Tales abound of drunken climbings-in through the windows of the ground-floor flats.

Tanning was hard work – out in the freezing cold, with the terrible smell from a cocktail of rotting flesh, chemicals and lime soaked into your clothes. Urine was used to remove the hair from animal skins, so some families would all piss into the same pot and sell their offerings to the tannery – the origins of the phrase "piss poor". If you couldn't afford said receptacle, then you "didn't have a pot to piss in".

Today the Dean Village is a far more fragrant affair, and Well Court has been perfectly restored by Edinburgh World Heritage. Go through the courtyard to the river's edge and you'll find Sydney Mitchell's stone water font. And hiding behind a large tree trunk, you'll find a picnic table where you can watch the Water of Leith stream by and admire Nick Hortin's balancing stones (see overleaf).

NEARBY

Just across the stone bridge from Well Court are two stones, built into the wall of the former granary on Bell's Brae. The image is of two bakers' paddles, crossed and bearing cakes; above them are two cake-loving cherubic faces. The inscription below reads, "God bless the Baxters of Edinburgh uho bult this hous 1675" [*sic*].

BALANCING STONES

❸

Water of Leith, Dean Village
• Viewable 24 hrs when river level low. Free

*Balancing
act*

A strange phenomenon started to occur in the Water of Leith in the early summer of 2015. Small stone turrets began to emerge out of the water, as if the riverbed rocks had decided to perform an amazing circus act, climbing on top of each other and balancing precariously – perhaps in a dramatic plea for help, or maybe in an attempt to catch the eye of passing festival programmers.

Locals started to notice them piling up near the bridge behind Well Court (see previous page), and further downstream towards St Bernard's Well. Images of the rock stacks started to appear on facebook and instagram. Who was making these stalagmitic works of art?

And then Nick Hortin was spotted, wading waste deep in the water, slowly and carefully placing one stone on top of another – and the mystery was solved. Nick, a social worker and part-time podiatrist, has lived on the river in the Dean Village since 2007. He's the kind of guy who likes to make things with his hands, and he has always had an affinity with water: he and his son are keen kayakers, and his garden is filled with colourful sea canoes. But these stone sculptures are an altogether more meditative transaction with the water.

The idea wasn't his: he'd seen a poster of some stone stacks by the Canadian artist Michael Grab and they'd inspired him to try. He had a pair of waist waders that someone had thrown out and he'd thought they might come in handy one day. Seven years later and they were the very thing he needed.

The art is not just to stack wide, flat stones with lots of contact points and easy stability, but to select ones which look unfeasible and then find the balancing point. You get better at it the more you do it. Sometimes Nick takes fifteen minutes to find it. The process is so absorbing, so focused, it becomes strangely relaxing. Some of the towers last only a couple of hours before the river washes them away, others have survived a couple of months. You can only really build them when the river is low, so you won't see many around in the winter months. But when the water level returns to just under 1 metre, Nick will be out there again, painstakingly building his gravity towers.

PUMP HOUSE OF ST BERNARD'S WELL

Water of Leith walkway between Saunders Street and the Dean Bridge
Nearest postcode: EH3 6TU
• Pump house open on occasion: check Dean Village website for alerts
• Admission free
• www.deanvillage.org
• Buses: 24, 29, 36, 42

> *A celestial vault*

Most Edinburgh folk have strolled past St Bernard's Well, the romantic pillared temple standing proudly on the edge of the Water of Leith, just upstream from Stockbridge. But what many don't realise is that on special days you can enter the pump house below, and discover a magical jewelled interior like something out of the Arabian Nights.

The Roman rotunda itself was built in 1789 by the rather eccentric Lord Gardenstone, who was quite a drinker and had an "extreme fondness for pigs", apparently keeping one in his bed for warmth. Gardenstone had just returned from a Grand Tour of Italy and he commissioned Alexander Nasmyth's design (based on the Temple of Vesta in Tivoli) to house the mineral spring that had been discovered by three schoolboys in 1760. Gardenstone believed its waters cured pretty much everything, though apparently it had an "odious twang of hydrogen gas" and tasted like "the washings from a foul gun barrel".

A coade stone statue (see p. 242) of Hygieia, Goddess of Health, with a snake feeding from her medicine bowl, stood at the centre of the open temple top. But she was so often used as target practice that she had to be replaced by a marble statue in 1887, when the new owner, local publisher William Nelson, had the entire place restored. You can see his plaque outside, next to the bricked-up entrance to what was once the well-keeper's hovel. It was Nelson who commissioned Thomas Bonnar to create a "celestial vault" inside, though sadly he died the same year as this wonderful design was completed.

Tiny golden mosaic stars pierce the mosaic blue sky which stretches across the steeply domed mosaic ceiling. At the centre, a golden Helios sun radiates out mosaic beams of entwining jewelled snakeskin circles, reaching down the walls to meet a terracotta and cream mosaic meander pattern. Below is a mosaic dado skirt of snakes, amphoras, lanterns and olive branches.

The floor is similarly patterned in more sober grey and white marble. At the centre is a pedestal with a lion's mouth ready to spout hand-cranked water into a basin below. On top is a beautifully carved antique amphora with snakes seething over the lid.

The inscription *"Bibendo valebis"* tells you: "By drinking you will be well." And if you're brave enough to test your taste for gassy gun washings, Edinburgh World Heritage recently restored the building and the pump is working again.

HIGH HORSES

Horse, Rider, Eagle: corner of Henderson Place Lane and Silvermills, Edinburgh EH3 5BF
• Buses: 24, 29, 36, 42
Horse and Rider: Rutland Court, Fountainbridge, Edinburgh EH3 8EY
• Buses: 3, 4, 22, 25, 30, 33, 44, 61
• Tram stop: West End
• Both viewable 24 hrs
• Free

Alchemy in action

Silvermills, the area below St Stephen Street in Stockbridge, apparently got its name because it was the medieval location of the experimental alchemical laboratories of James IV or V, both enthusiastic dabblers in mystic metallurgy. Half a millennium later, housing developers transformed the location into luxury flats. Out of which was distilled a great bronze sculpture, since all large construction projects were required to fund public art under the "percent for art" scheme.

So, slap bang in the middle of the upmarket housing scheme is a larger-than-life sculpture by Edinburgh-born Eoghan Bridge. A great horse strains as a naked rider grabs onto the claws of a flying eagle and attempts lift-off. It's not on any through road – the winding medieval street layout was retained – so very few people pass by. And despite the melodrama of the action so close to their kitchen windows, many residents hardly notice the piece. Several people I questioned didn't even know it was there.

On the other side of town, in the Fountainbridge financial district (where they practise a different kind of algorithm-based alchemy), another of Eoghan's horses performs a dramatic act on the pedestrian bridge leading over the Western Approach Road. The bronze beast squats on its hind legs and rears up as the rider pulls back its head, hard. The 1992 sculpture was the first equestrian statue to be erected in Edinburgh in seventy years, its predecessors being nearly all military.

Despite their heads being twisted in Guernica-style poses, Bridge's horses seem to be working in collaboration with their riders. Both sculptures appear to be part of some kind of rodeo circus act, or an equine stunt scene from a Western where our hero manages to escape his pursuers by an extraordinary feat of skill and bravery. The artist's studio shelves are crammed with maquettes of horses in the most ungainly poses, sometimes balancing comically on top of their riders. His most recent foray is into bulls: surely some financial institution should be in the market for that.

JAMES CLERK MAXWELL FOUNDATION

14 India Street, Edinburgh EH3 6EZ
- www.clerkmaxwellfoundation.org/html/birthplace.html
- Email: 14indiastreet@gmail.com
- Viewing by appointment Tues afternoons and Fri mornings
- Buses: 24, 29, 42

A magnetic museum

James Clerk Maxwell was one of the most important physicists of all time – up there with Einstein and Newton – and yet he is hardly a household name. In 1865 he discovered that light is a wave which has electrical and magnetic parts to it – a huge leap in understanding, which led directly to the development of radio communications such as radar, radio, TV and mobile phones. Einstein even said, "The special theory of relativity owes its origins to Maxwell's equations of the electromagnetic field."

And that world-changing brilliant mind originated in this Edinburgh New Town house. Maxwell was born here in 1831 and though his rather wealthy parents soon moved him out to their country estate in the Borders, he returned here aged 10 to study at the Edinburgh Academy and later at the University of Edinburgh.

A hundred years after his death, the James Clerk Maxwell Foundation was established and vowed that if JCM's house ever came on the market they would buy it. But when it eventually came up for sale, it was way beyond their means: local properties were particularly sought after by the legal profession as they fell within the range of the pushcart that hand delivered legal briefs to all the barristers. But due to advances in communications which have their origins in Maxwell's equations – faxes and emails – barristers were able to move further away and the price of 14 India Street dropped just enough for the foundation to be able to purchase it in 1993.

They stuffed the house full of everything Clerk Maxwellian they could find. Many of these items were touchingly personal: a 'dynamical top' he used to demonstrate 'precession' using his theory of colour mixing; his paper on Oval Curves, which he wrote aged 14 and was presented to the Royal Society of Edinburgh; the three colour plates he used to project the first photographic colour image; a chair embroidered by his aunt with an almost digital design representing light as a wave; and drawings of him as a child by his cousin, the artist Jemima Blackburn, one of the most popular illustrators of her time. One drawing shows the two of them "tubbing" around a loch in a pair of wooden barrels, James looking very serious – perhaps thinking about the waves his oar was creating. Apparently he was a very inquisitive child, prone to driving adults crazy with his questioning of everything. Thankfully, they didn't put him off.

If you're interested in exploring further, there is a great free JCM quiz trail to follow on your phone. Download the global treasure app: www.globaltreasureapp.com

LIBRARY OF MISTAKES

4a Wemyss Place Mews, Edinburgh EH3 6DN
• www.libraryofmistakes.com
• Email: keeper@libraryofmistakes.com
• Open Mon–Fri 9am–5pm. The library has the same holidays as the London Stock Exchange
• Buses: 19, 29, 42

"Not rocket science"

An inauspicious door at the end of Wemyss Place Mews displays a sign, "The Library of Mistakes", with the M replaced by a descending stock market arrow – a clue as to what kind of world-shaking mistakes we're dealing with. Upstairs you will find a beautiful cosy little library, lined with books on the practical history of financial markets. There are no tombs of mathematical equations here. Keeper of the Library and Errorist-in-chief Russell Napier is emphatic that the library is an antidote to the illusion that economics is all about hard sums. Economists, he says, have what is termed "physics envy" – they're desperate for economics to be acknowledged as a science, with solid mathematical rules, when in actuality it is a social science, dictated by human behaviour and historical patterns.

Even if financial gain isn't your personal pursuit, you can still book in and use the place for your own reading pleasure. But it's hard not to get drawn in. Lining the walls and the mantelpieces are amusing souvenirs of past financial ineptitudes. A portrait of Charles Ponzi, the only man to have a fraudulent investment scheme named after him. A British Leyland keyring, pointing to the disastrous merger of Britain's main car manufacturers in the late sixties. A mini American football plastered in the sponsor's logo "Peregrine Hong Kong Sevens" … but the arrogant investment bank had collapsed before the tournament even took place. A pack of playing cards with images themed on the first stock market crash, caused by the 1720 "South Sea Bubble". A framed logo of bankrupt American energy company Enron – the poster boys of creative accounting, whose motto read, "The possibilities are endless".

A more local reference is a sketch of the Scots feverishly boarding the ship bound for Darien, Scotland's ill-fated attempt to found a colony in 1698. Unfortunately, the Promised Land was an uninhabitable disease-ridden stretch of Panama. Twenty-five per cent of Scotland's money perished with those foolhardy colonisers. The investors, mainly landed gentry, were offered a bail-out if they voted for the Act of Union, hence Robert Burns' line "bought and sold for English gold". Much of this same money was used to start up a new bank, the Royal Bank of Scotland, which would go on to head an even bigger financial disaster. Will we never learn?

MASONIC LODGE NO. 1

⑧

19 Hill Street, Edinburgh EH2 3JP
• www.lodgeofedinburgh.org.uk
• Tel: 0131 225 7294
• Buses: 24, 29, 42

***Ciphers
deciphered***

With its scroll-topped blue pillars and bold lettering, the door of 19 Hill Street is a distinctive entrance to the Masonic Lodge No. 1. Despite being a Georgian town house, it bears the name "Mary's Chapel" as that was the original location of the lodge in Niddry's Wynd – just off the Cowgate, until the street was demolished in 1787 to make way for the South Bridge (see p. 41). The lodge is designated No. 1 in Scotland and it may well be the oldest Freemason lodge in the world. References are made to it in 1504 and it holds minutes of the oldest Masonic meeting on 31 July 1599, making it the world's oldest Masonic document.

This was the first lodge to admit speculative Freemasons, i.e. members who were not builders. Some think the first such member (admitted in 1600) was Sir Thomas Boswell, a distant ancestor of Samuel Johnson's biographer; others

think he may have just been signed in for a meeting. But there is clear proof that in 1641 the natural philosopher Robert Moray and the Scottish army colonel Henry Mainwaring were officially initiated as honorary members. Other famous initiates were the Prince of Wales in 1870, and after him Kings Edward VII and VIII (the one who abdicated).

If you look further up at the door, you will see an even more distinctive embellishment above the window. An encircled star, with a series of numbers and symbols, has been boldly carved into the stone. The four numbers on the outside of the circle are simply the date 1893, the year it was proposed by Dr George Dickson, the Master of this lodge. His design comprised a hexalpha, a star made up of two opposing equilateral triangles (see following double-page spread for more information on the history and symbolism of the hexalpha). At their centre is a fiery G, the symbol of the Great Architect, i.e. God, radiating his power. The top triangle represents the spirit, the lower one matter, and their layout shows they are in balanced opposition: "As above, so below". They are surrounded by a circle of perfect universal harmony. This all tells the trained eye that, due to the work of the lodge, all is well in the world.

Around the outside of the star are the letters "LEMCN⁰1", which is a simple abbreviation for "Lodge of Edinburgh, Mary's Chapel No. 1". The other Pictish rune 16 symbols are the personal signature marks of each of the officials of the Lodge of Scotland at the time, four of them Grand Lodge Office Bearers. George Dickson himself appears at the top as an H with a rising sun above it.

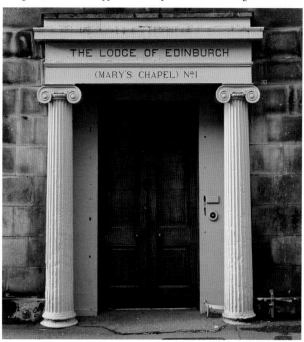

THE STAR HEXAGRAM: A MAGICAL TALISMAN?

The hexagram – also known as the Star of David or the Shield of David – comprises two interlaced equilateral triangles, one pointing upwards and the other downwards. It symbolises the combination of man's spiritual and human nature. The six points correspond to the six directions in space (north, south, east and west, together with zenith and nadir) and also refer to the complete universal cycle of the six days of creation (the seventh day being when the Creator rested). Hence, the hexagram became the symbol of the macrocosm (its six angles of 60° totalling 360°) and of the union between mankind and its creator. If, as laid down in the Old Testament (*Deuteronomy* 6:4–9), the hexagram (*mezuzah* in Hebrew) is often placed at the entrance to a Jewish home, it was also adopted as an amulet by Christians and Muslims. So it is far from being an exclusively Jewish symbol. In both the Koran (38:32 et seq.) and *The Thousand and One Nights*, it is described as an indestructible talisman that affords God's blessing and offers total protection against the spirits of the natural world, the djinns. The hexagram also often appears in the windows and pediments of Christian churches, as a symbolic reference to the universal soul. In this case, that soul is represented by Christ – or, sometimes, by the pair of Christ (upright triangle) and the Virgin (inverted triangle); the result of the interlacing of the two is God the Father Almighty. The hexagram is also found in the mediated form of a lamp with six branches or a six-section rose window.

Although present in the synagogue of Capernaum (third century AD), the hexagram does not really make its appearance in rabbinical literature until 1148 – in the *Eshkol Hakofer* written by the Karaite* scholar Judah Ben Elijah. In Chapter 242 its mystical and apotropaic (evil-averting) qualities are described, with the actual words then often being engraved on amulets: "And the names of the seven angels were written on the *mazuzah*: The Everlasting will protect you and this symbol called the Shield of David contains, at the end of the *mezuzah*, the written name of all the angels."

In the thirteenth century the hexagram also became an attribute of one of the seven magic names of Metatron, the angel of the divine presence associated with the archangel Michael (head of the heavenly host and the closest to God the Father).

The identification of Judaism with the Star of David began in the Middle Ages. In 1354 King Karel IV of Bohemia granted the Jewish community of Prague the privilege of putting the symbol on their banner. The Jews embroidered a gold star on a red background to form a standard that became known as the Flag of King David (*Maghen David*) and was adopted as the official symbol of Jewish synagogues. By the nineteenth century, the symbol had spread throughout the Jewish community. Jewish mysticism has it that the origin of the hexagram was directly linked with the flowers that adorn the *menorah***: irises with six petals. For those who believe this origin, the hexagram came directly from the hands of the God of Israel, the six-petal iris not only reassembling the Star of David in general form but also being associated with the people of Israel in the *Song of Songs*.

As well as offering protection, the hexagram was believed to have magical powers. This reputation originates in the famous *Clavicula Salomonis* (Key of Solomon), a grimoire (textbook of magic) attributed to Solomon himself but, in all likelihood, produced during the Middle Ages. The anonymous texts probably came from one of the numerous Jewish schools of the Kabbalah that then existed in Europe, for the work is clearly inspired by the teachings of the Talmud and the Jewish faith. The *Clavicula* contains a collection of thirty-six pentacles (themselves symbols rich in magic and esoteric significance) which were intended to enable communication between the physical world and the different levels of the soul. There are various versions of the text, in numerous translations, and the content varies between them. However, most of the surviving texts date from the sixteenth and seventeenth centuries – although there is a Greek translation dating from the fifteenth.

In Tibet and India, the Buddhists and Hindus read this universal symbol of the hexagram in terms of the creator and his creation, while the Brahmins hold it to be the symbol of the god Vishnu. Originally, the two triangles were in green (upright triangle) and red (inverted triangle). Subsequently, these colours became black and white, the former representing the spirit, the latter the material world. For the Hindus, the upright triangle is associated with Shiva, Vishnu and Brahma (corresponding to the Christian God the Father, Son and Holy Ghost). The Son (Vishnu) can be seen to always occupy the middle position, being the intercessor between things divine and things earthly.

gara'im or *bnei mikra*: "he who follows the Scriptures". Karaism is a branch of Judaism that defends the sole authority of the Hebrew Scripture as the source of divine revelation, thus repudiating oral tradition.
**Menorah – the multibranched candelabra used in the rituals of Judaism. The arms of the seven-branched menorah, one of the oldest symbols of the Jewish faith, represent the seven archangels before the Throne of God: Michael, Gabriel, Samuel, Raphael, Zadkiel, Anael and Kassiel.

WHITE STUFF CHANGING ROOMS

89 George Street, Edinburgh EH2 3ES
• Tel: 0131 300 0330
• www.whitestuff.com
• Open Mon–Wed & Fri–Sat 9.30am–6pm, Thurs 9.30am–7pm, Sun 11am–5pm
• Buses: 10, 11, 12, 16, 24, 29, 42 (Lothian), 100 (Airlink)

Narnia interior

A s you march along past the Edinburgh branch of the White Stuff at No. 89 George Street, you might think that you're passing just another high-street fashion shop. But nestling at the back of this branch is a door into another world. In fact, many doors and many worlds. Because the White Stuff changing rooms are a work of closet art.

Head upstairs, via the stairs – or better, the lift (painted with the giant JH Lynch kitsch sixties nymph print). Female shoppers who wish to size up some style stumble across a corridor lined with shallow wardrobes, somewhat resembling a Leith Walk second-hand furniture shop. But pull open a creaky, hinged door and you won't find a rack of dusty coat hangers and a yellowing newspaper, but a tiny individually-themed room. Step inside and trial-spin your frock in a 1940s kitchen larder, lined with packs of Bird's custard mix and tins of marrowfat peas. See how big your butt looks in a room stuffed full with cuddly toys. Or rest that weary bot on a toilet seat, housed in a lime tiled bathroom complete with a supply of loo rolls.

The range was designed by AMD Interior Architects, but a few of the cubicles, like the outer space themed one, were dreamed up by school kids for a competition. You can see their original designs pinned to the back of the doors.

Sometimes the White Stuff have exhibitions and other fun events; they even have a 'meet and make area' where you can learn a craft and sip locally-made

herbal infusions from a vintage teacup. There is sure to be something exciting happening during the Edinburgh Festival. But even when there's nothing official going on, you can still pop in and hang out in the changing rooms, they're a fringe show in themselves.

MASONIC MUSEUM

The Grand Lodge of Scotland, Freemasons Hall, 96 George Street,
Edinburgh EH2 3DH
• Tel: 0131 225 5577
• www.grandlodgescotland.com
• Open Mon–Fri 9.30am–3.30pm. Tours of building & museum at 10am
and 2pm
• Admission free, though donations welcome
• Buses: 10, 11, 12, 16, 24, 29, 42

A symbolic selection

For all the rumours of secrecy and exclusivity, the only barrier to visiting the Masonic Museum in Edinburgh is making sure you visit on a weekday. If you promise not to pester them with questions about the Da Vinci Code or Satanic goat rituals, you can just drop in on the two rooms housing the eclectic collection of Masonic memorabilia. Even if you're a woman.

Freemasonry in Scotland is recorded as far back as 1491. At the time, all craft workers – bakers, brewers, silversmiths, etc. – formed incorporations to protect their crafts and pass on their secret recipes and skills which, in a pre-copyright era, were the basis of their livelihoods. Those involved in the building trade – architects, engineers, stonemasons, etc. – did the same. However, as a way of raising extra cash, they allowed non-professionals to attend their gatherings, where they taught morality and conducted ceremonies. To protect their trade secrets from this Masonic-lite membership, the Freemasons created secret lodges for the inner core, where they would pass on their Pythagorean equations and techniques. Partly to keep these secret and partly because many members were illiterate, a symbolic language was developed along with ritualised methods of learning, like question and answer catechisms.

It is this symbolic language which you will see adorning the ceremonial objects in the museum. Collections of ornamental glasses, knives, silver trowels for laying foundation stones, aprons, clocks and medals, referred to as "jewels", are all decorated with compasses, set squares and slide rules. There are also images referencing the Masons' moral code – all-seeing eyes, brothers in arms, innocent lambs. The collections come not just from Scotland but from all over the world, including the jewels of the Grand Lodge of Czechoslovakia, donated in 1936, before its members were exterminated by Hitler.

And there are celebrity members here, including Robert Burns himself: you can see his signature on the membership book, his (rather charred) apron, and a painting of him being inaugurated as Poet Laureate of the Canongate Lodge in 1787. Another portrait shows his friend George Washington on his inauguration into the Scottish Lodge in Virginia, 1758. But you won't find much about Dan Brown or Rosslyn Chapel here, and if it's the Holy Grail you're after, you'll need to trot on.

"BEACHCOMBER"

BT Exchange, 139–157 Rose Street, Edinburgh EH2 4LS
- Open 24 hrs
- Admission free
- Buses: 10, 11, 12, 13, 16, 22, 25

*Poetry
in ocean*

The BT Exchange was always a bit of an empty stretch on the westernmost block of Rose Street; pub crawlers who have worked their way through a dozen bars become disorientated when they don't find another within ten paces. Shoppers turn their backs on the building's blocked-out windows and stray to the other side to browse shop fronts filled with engagement rings, ballet shoes and Havana cigars.

But now there's something inhabiting the archways of the old telephone exchange which might encourage them to reconsider such consumerist values: in 2013 the words of George MacKay Brown's poem "Beachcomber" were illustrated by artist Astrid Jaekel. Her hand-cut paper design was lasered, imperfections and all, into steel panels by Pentland Precision Engineering, then powder-coated in russet, to create a surprisingly delicate façade – like a paper doily turned to rusted metal.

Jaekel spent a long time searching for a poem that would be accessible, not too verbose, and with a structure to suit seven windows. The Orcadian poet's words catalogue the daily findings of a beachcomber during a week of seaside foraging. The lines swirl in the waves with shoals of fish and sea-washed treasure. Look carefully and you'll find bobbing among them a few extra-poetic additions, like a pub lamp, a telephone and a portrait of the poet himself.

The boot that the beachcomber finds on Monday is not an old docker's, as you might expect, but a sexy knee-high FMB, conjuring up the 1960s, when this street was strutted by ladies of the night. Weaving among them were Stella Cartwright and her coterie of besotted poets: Hugh MacDiarmid, Norman MacCaig, Sorley MacLean et al. had been drinking and debating poetry here since the '50s. Young, sexy and likely to drink you under the table, Cartwright was muse and lover to most of them, but MacKay Brown really fell for her. Despite her bohemian lifestyle, they became engaged. Even after their relationship ended, he wrote a poem for her every year on her birthday … a tradition that didn't last long because she died at only 47, having sold MacKay Brown's letters to pay for the drink that killed her. Death was never far from his poems – the beachcomber's hard life gives him a loud cough, and when he finds a spar of timber, he knows that next winter it could just as easily become a coffin as a bed. Think on, dear shopper. You never know what the sea will wash up for you next.

NEARBY

Look carefully at the green flower boxes towards the Castle Street end and you'll see more of George MacKay Brown's words, this time cataloguing a week in the life of "The Hawk". And at the South Charlotte Street end, the side of the Roxburgh Hotel has a space for a changing poem every season.

LIBRARY ROOM AT DEBENHAMS

First floor, 109 Princes Street, Edinburgh EH2 3AA
- Tel: 0844 561 6161
- www.debenhams.com
- Admission free during store opening hours, see website for details
- Buses: 3, 10, 11, 15, 16, 19, 30, 31, 33, 37, 41, 104, 113
- Tram stop: Princes Street

Gladstone vs. Disraeli

The womenswear department of Debenhams is not exactly where you would expect to find an antique book library dedicated to former Prime Minister William Gladstone. But go through the arch with "Through to Library Room & Personal shopper" emblazoned on it and there it is, complete with ornate bookcases, Victorian fireplace, statues of reclining deer and a marble bust of Gladstone himself, looking pretty grumpy to be stuck behind the sparkly evening dresses and turquoise jeggings.

Or maybe it's because his great political rival, Benjamin Disraeli, is just across the non-political floor, typically upstaging him with a stained-glass window triptych of three women representing politics, empire and literature. Between them is a lavish café spangled with gold acanthus-leaf-topped red marble pillars. The reason for all the opulent incongruity is this: Debenhams is spread across two buildings which were, from the end of the 19th century, the oddest of neighbours: the Liberal and Conservative clubs.

Gladstone and Disraeli really hated each other. The Conservative party had recently split over Robert Peel's reform of the Corn Laws, and the two were on opposite sides: Disraeli had led the rebellion against Peel (Gladstone's hero) which brought down his government. Gladstone and his fellow Peelites had defected to the Whigs and formed the new Liberal party.

Disraeli was a flamboyant dandy. Oscar Wilde was a fan; his *Picture of Dorian Gray* was partly inspired by Disraeli's first novel, *Vivian Grey*, mainly written to get himself out of debt. He charmed Queen Victoria and crowned her Empress of India, while she made him Earl of Beaconsfield. Gladstone, on the other hand, was more sober and serious; his only foray into fashion was to have a heavy hinged leather bag named after him. He never got on with Queen Vic, who complained that he addressed her as if she were a public meeting.

Gladstone served as prime minister right up until the age of 84, earning the nickname "G.O.M.", or Grand Old Man. (Disraeli preferred "God's Only Mistake".) Gladstone said of Disraeli, "In past times the Tory party had principles by which it would and did stand, for bad and for good. All this Dizzy destroyed." But Disraeli gave a quip worthy of Wilde himself: "If Gladstone fell into the Thames, it would be a misfortune. But if someone fished him out again, that would be a calamity."

MUSEUM COLLECTIONS CENTRE

10 Broughton Market, Edinburgh EH3 6NU
• Tel: 0131 556 9536
• www.edinburghmuseums.org.uk/Venues/Museum-Collections-Centre
• Access by appointment or at 2pm on first Tuesday of the month:
advance booking advisable
• Free but donations welcomed
• Buses: 8, 10, 11, 12, 16, 26, 41, 44
• Tram stop: York Place

Behind
the scenes
at the museum

Edinburgh City Council's museums own over 200,000 objects between them – too many to be on permanent display, so the overflow gets sorted and stored at the Museum Collections Centre. Visiting the place is like going backstage at the biggest, most random film production ever mounted. Trying to work out a narrative structure would be taxing for even the most experienced Hollywood script doctor.

What story could incorporate a Roman Vestal Virgin statue, the 18th-century St Giles clock mechanism, a small copse of hooded hairdryers, a rack of King's Theatre panto costumes, a 1970s toddler-sized Tippy Tumbles doll ("She's tricky … she's flippy!") and a bank of vintage televisions? Perhaps you've accidentally walked into Terry Gilliam's brain …

You'll be shown round the neural pathways by one of the in-house conservators, who are experts on all things monumental and also helped restore many of the pieces you see around the city. You can get answers to all your best monumental questions: no, the pig's ear story about the statue of Bucephalus outside the City Chambers isn't true, though sculptor Sir John Steell must have been pretty peeved at not being paid for fifty years.

There's quite a menagerie here. If you miss the plump pigeons from Elm Row, they're roosting under this roof. It was in this workshop that the wonderful Wardrop's Court dragons were restored to their turquoise and gold. If you're lucky on your visit, something interesting will be being brushed up, sanded down or restuffed in the workshop.

But the most fascinating items are the less glamorous everyday objects in the social history section, cataloguing the changes in domestic and work life. Gadgets of the past, like Bakelite radios, cast-iron typewriters and enormous 1950s prams. Signage from shops on the edges of living memory: William Leith & Co., J. Williamson & Son, John Herdman & Sons. All ready for their close-up at a museum near you, whenever they call "Action".

ARCHIVIST'S GARDEN

- Open daily: 9am–5pm
- Admission free
- Buses: 1, 3, 4, 7, 14, 15, 19, 22, 25, 29, 30, 31, 33, 34, 37, 49, 104, 113

Garden of collective memory

I f you ever need to get away from the chaos of the tourist/commuter/shopper intersection between Princes Street, the Bridges and Waverley, the Archivist's Garden is a good place to slip into sideways. Lying in a gap between the General Register House and the New Register House, the garden is filled with plants, benches and circling walkways.

The two Register Houses that cloak it from view contain the painstakingly ordered archive files that record all Scotland's births, deaths and marriages. But in the intervening garden, banks of flowers, grasses and trees are catalogued, not according to a linear, chronological or alphabetical system, but flowing in the disorganised and associative way in which the brain holds memories. While the architecture of the two buildings is one of perfect symmetry and classical composition, the Archivist's Garden weaves its bands of planting to mirror the twisting contours of the brain, with its irregular patterns and idiosyncratic connections.

The planting was curated by the Royal Botanic Garden Edinburgh's David Mitchell, to represent Scotland's collective memory: its folklore, its famous folk, its heraldry and tartans. Strangely, there are exactly 57 varieties of plants – perhaps Heinz baked beans are also embedded in Scotland's collective unconscious.

The red rose, the rowan, the thistle and wild heather are of course part of the mix, but not all the plants have such easily readable Scots associations. There are plants which were collected by famous Scots botanists, like the beautiful African Blue Lily (*Agapanthus africanus*), which was brought back in the late 1700s by Aberdeen-born plant collector Francis Masson. And plants which are associated with birth, marriage and death, like the almond tree which flowers so early that it has long been a symbol of fertility – sugared almonds are still given at christenings, and almond flowers are scattered at weddings. There are also plants like meadowsweet and silver birch, which were used to dye wool for tartans and tweeds.

So if you've spent half the day in the ScotlandsPeople Centre trying to track down your family tree to no avail, come outside and forget it all in this garden of collective memory. As Robert Louis Stevenson (who is also remembered here) wrote, "Do not judge each day by the harvest you reap, but the seeds you sow."

TO PRESERVE
THE JEWEL OF LIBERTY
IN THE FRAMEWORK OF
FREEDOM
ABRAHAM LINCOLN

IN MEMORY OF SCOTTISH-AMERICAN SOLDIERS.

STATUE OF ABRAHAM LINCOLN

Old Calton Graveyard, 27 Waterloo Place, Edinburgh EH1 3BQ
- Open 24 hrs
- Admission free
- 5-min. walk from Waverley Station
- Buses: 6, 15, 25, 34, 34, 43, 45, 104, 113, X25, X26, X44

> *Edinburgh's shady past with slavery*

The Old Calton Graveyard is one of Edinburgh's most dramatic cemeteries: its darkened gateway in the high stone wall of Waterloo Place leads up to a platform opening onto a wide precipice with impressive views over the city.

The graveyard is stuffed full of Edinburgh's greats – philosopher David Hume, architect Thomas Hamilton, actor William Woods. But standing among them is one very notable non-resident. The statue of Abraham Lincoln is the only monument to the American Civil War outside the United States. Erected in 1893, it was the first effigy of an American president beyond their shores. Here Abe stands dressed in the same three-piece suit and bowtie combo as he wears in the Washington memorial, in his hand the Thirteenth Amendment. At his feet is a freed slave, one hand stretched out in praise, the other resting on a book. The inscription is a quote from Lincoln's writings: "*To preserve the jewel of liberty in the framework of freedom*".

The monument honours those Scots who joined the American fight for the abolition of slavery and the union of North and South. Six are named here, including Sergeant Major MacEwan, whose wife's campaign for her war widow's pension led to the realisation that the soldiers' sacrifices deserved recognition.

A SUGAR COATING

It is indeed a noble cause for which they fought, but rather less commemorated is Edinburgh's shady past association with slavery – though the connection with the plantations can be traced in names like Jamaica Street, India Street and Sugarhouse Close. Edinburgh had at least six "sugar-houses", where the sugar harvested by slaves was refined. In 1817 a third of the slaves in Jamaica were owned by Scots. Dundas Street is named after Henry Dundas, who campaigned against William Wilberforce's 1833 anti-slavery bill, and without whose "skillful obstructions the slave trade would have been abolished in 1796, if not 1792". James Gillespie, who built Edinburgh's famous high school, made his fortune from the tobacco trade. Sir John Gladstone, father of Prime Minister William Gladstone, was the Leith-born owner of ten plantations whose slaves revolted against his cruelty. West Indian slaves were even brought to Jock's Lodge by their owners to be taught a trade so they could be sold at a higher profit. So as you admire the commendable cause marked by the Civil War memorial, remember that this city was not always fighting on the right side!

BRONZE DOORS OF ST ANDREW'S HOUSE

2 Regent Road, Edinburgh EH1 3DG
• Viewable when building is closed at weekends, and weekdays
10pm–6.30am
• Buses: 6, 15, 22, 25, 34, 45, 104, 113
• 10-min. walk from Waverley Station

Behind
closed doors

St Andrew's House, on the side of Calton Hill, is one of the city's most stunning pieces of modernist architecture. It was built in 1938 to the designs of Thomas S. Tait, the Paisley-born architect who also created the Art Deco pylons of Sydney Harbour Bridge.

The exterior of the building is crammed with beautifully crafted detail: the pillar caps are carved with thistles, roses and shamrocks, and the figures looking down from above the tall windows represent each of the government building's six original departments: Architecture, Statecraft, Health, Agriculture, Fisheries and Education.

But one impressive feature remains hidden from view for most passers-by: the great bronze doors are only visible when the building is shut. Nine feet wide and 12 feet high (approx. 2.7 x 3.7 metres), they were designed by the sculptor Walter Gilbert and modelled by his son Donald. The panels depict four Scottish saints around the St Andrew's Cross: St Columba, St Ninian, St Magnus and St Kentigern, each representing a different Scottish ethnic group.

St Columba, who came from Ireland to the west coast of Scotland and banished the Loch Ness monster, represents the Gaels. St Ninian, who converted the south-west of Scotland, represents the Anglo-Saxons. St Magnus of Orkney, who was forced to take refuge in Scotland after refusing to take part in a Viking raid, represents his Viking blood. And the Picts are represented by St Kentigern, aka St Mungo, a missionary who became patron saint of Glasgow (though his mother came from Haddington, where she had been thrown from the heights of Traprain Law by her father as punishment for being raped).

Each of these saints was vying for the position of Scotland's patron saint, but in a bold act of internationalism, St Andrew was chosen at the Declaration of Arbroath in 1320, thus unifying the rival Scottish factions.

You'll find St Andrew by the door handles, fishing in the Sea of Galilee as Jesus calls him, saying, "And I will make you fishers of men" – the words inscribed on either side of the great thistle handles. Just under Andrew's armpit is the keyhole. A golden key was created especially for King George VI to unlock at the opening ceremony, but the Second World War broke out the month before and so the key was never used. It is kept in a display case in the Permanent Secretary's office inside – you can only go in on Doors Open Day (September), when places get booked up well in advance.

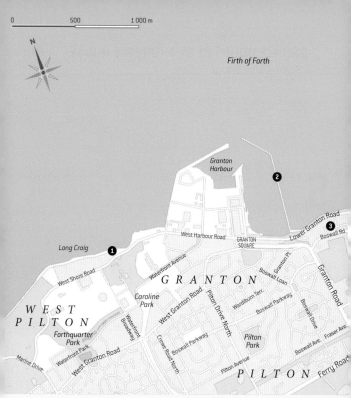

NORTH - LEITH

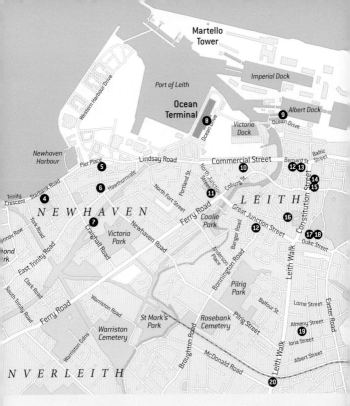

PROMENADE RUBBINGS TRAIL

Edinburgh Promenade, Granton to Cramond
• Buses: 24, 47 (Granton); 16, 27, 47 (Silverknowes); 41 (Cramond)

*Coastal
reliefs*

The coastal walk from Granton harbour to Cramond is about an hour long. There is a beautiful view of the Forth as you move from the fishing port of Granton, behind the Pilton gas towers, into the open space of Gypsy Brae, the shores of Silverknowes beach and on to Roman Cramond.

With such views to distract you, it's easy to miss the series of small plinths dotted along the railings. There are currently nine in total, each topped with a postcard-sized brass plaque sporting a raised design inviting you to rub and replicate designs by local schoolchildren from three different schools: Pirniehall Primary, Davidson's Mains and Cramond Primary.

The reliefs are the work of artist Kate Ive, who has a studio in the Edinburgh Sculpture Workshop just along the coast in Newhaven. Ive was hot off the press after being selected as the British Art Medal Society's new medallist, which meant she had studied all the right techniques at the Royal Academy and the Royal Mint. She etched the winning sketches into plaster blocks, made a silicon mould and then poured hot wax into that negative. The next step was for Powderhall Bronze foundry to cover the wax in clay slurry and bake it until the wax melted out. This produced the negative into which the melted bronze was finally poured.

The children had been encouraged to think about their environments and their local heritage. So near Granton harbour you'll find drawings of the local sea life and fishing industry, including a wonderful shoal of little fishes like tiny floating fried eggs. Near Silverknowes you'll find images of the local buildings, including Lauriston Castle. And at Cramond you'll find pictures of the Roman heritage and the iron mill. Just pack your paper and crayons and you can take home your very own print collection.

GRANTON HARBOUR HUTS

2

Lower Granton Road, Edinburgh EH5 1EX
• Open 24 hrs
• Access free
• Bus: 16

Breakwater bothies

With Newhaven harbour being all malled up with superstores and royal yachts, Granton harbour is like stepping back in time. Gone are the fleets of fishing trawlers, the bustle of trains and the ice factory (where apparently ice cubes were first "invented"). The harbour is now mainly used by yacht clubs, rowers, a creeling boat and, now that the waters are cleaner, local wildlife: you can sometimes see seals sunning themselves on the pontoons in the middle of the harbour. The best time to visit is just after high tide.

Strolling down the half-mile-long eastern harbour wall, you will pass two large concrete bothies standing on stilts at the harbourside. Covered in imposing graffiti, they are now used by members of the street drinking fraternity to gather and share anecdotes, so they might not be the most desirable places to explore internally. But back in the 1930s they were part of a much healthier lifestyle. The first was a changing hut for the swimming club – a bunch of hardy swimmers who every day used to dive off the eastern breakwater and plough through the chill waters of the harbour and the Forth. When they returned to dry land, they would defrost in the hut over a wood fire – peer in and you'll see the chimney hole in the roof. The practice seemed to have died out, but recently a few brave swimmers have been spotted reviving the tradition.

The second breakwater bothy belonged to the yacht club, which had a flag pole and a cannon on top of the roof that was fired for the start of their races. During a May Week every two years, the harbour is filled with beautiful German ocean yachts which have raced from Heligoland to Granton, a fixture set up in 1969 to promote post-war friendship between Germany and Scotland and still going strong.

At the far end of the eastern breakwater lies the third (and smallest) hut. This houses the red port-hand navigation light for entering the harbour, powered by a solar panel on the top.

By contrast, on the opposite side of the bay is the middle pier, where you can see the oldest building in the harbour. This huge old stone warehouse, built in the early 1840s when the harbour opened, was one of four matching buildings. Now it's mainly a depository for pigeon droppings but it is known locally as the Gunpowder Store because that's what the British Navy used it for during the Napoleonic wars.

Legendary swimmer Ned Barnie from Portobello – who in 1950 was the first Scot to swim the English Channel, a year later the first man to swim it both directions, and who for twenty-eight years held the record of being the oldest person to swim the Channel – used to limber up by swimming from Granton harbour to Burntisland on the Fife coast. The 7-mile (11-km) swim took him four hours and twenty minutes.

CHALLENGER LODGE

St Columba's Hospice, 15 Boswall Road, Edinburgh EH5 3RW
- Tel: 0131 551 1381
- www.stcolumbashospice.org.uk/iona-cafe
- Email: info@stcolumbashospice.org.uk
- The lodge is viewable from the café, which is open to the public, but please be sensitive
- Iona Café open daily 8.30am–8.30pm
- Buses: 8, 14, 16

Heart of the hospice

St Columba's Hospice is a quietly amazing piece of modern architecture wrapped around a classical heart. This state-of-the-art facility, built in the grounds of a grand Georgian house, is designed to provide a calm and caring atmosphere for both patients and visitors. The outer layer of contemporary glass walkways, spacious and naturally lit wards and sandstone courtyard with vertical planted screens allow as much privacy or interactivity as the individual needs. With views over the sea or the internal garden, the sensitive architecture helps to connect patients with natural cycles and the idea of being part of a greater whole.

At the heart of the hospice, and visible through the sheltering glass, is the impressive neoclassical house called Challenger Lodge, which is now the administrative and fund-raising centre. It started life in 1825 as Wardie Lodge, built for Thomas Hope, an Edinburgh University Professor of Chemistry. Hope installed his niece Fanny in it, a pioneer gardener who inspired Gertrude Jekyll with her mixing of flower and vegetable planting.

The house became Challenger Lodge when it was bought by the oceanographer Sir John Murray in 1897; he named it after the ship in which he explored the great oceans of the world.

In 1929 the lodge was purchased by the Edinburgh Cripple and Invalid Children's Aid Society, which turned it into a residential school for children with disabilities caused by polio. They had occasional celebrity visitors, including Roy Rogers and Bob Hope. Seven minutes into a film entitled *The Chief's Half-Day* (www.movingimage.nls.uk/film/5905), you can even see footage of PC Willie Merrilees presenting the children with the dog who played Greyfriars Bobby.

A SHIP'S ANCHOR AND IRON RAILINGS FROM THE CUNARD LUXURY LINER, THE RMS *AQUITANIA*

Next door at 17 Boswell Road, the hospice runs an education centre for health professionals. In the garden is a ship's anchor which is thought to be that of HMS *Challenger* herself. The ornate black wrought-iron railings along the front were salvaged from the *Aquitania*, considered one of the most beautiful ships ever built.

STARBANK PARK

Starbank Road, Edinburgh EH5 3BX
- Open 24 hrs
- Admission free
- Buses: 11, 16

> *Hidden star of the Forth*

A s you drive along the water's edge between Newhaven and Granton harbours, you pass a steep banked garden. On the green slope is a large red flower bed planted in the shape of a star. Flanked by two yellow crescent moons, it is an eight-pointed "Star of the Sea", symbolising a ship's compass and the days when sailors would navigate the oceans by the stars. But it may have other meanings, as in traditional symbolism the octagram has particular significance for Christians, Masons, Wikans and Pagans: it represents, among other things, chaos, redemption, regeneration and the turn of the seasons.

What many admirers of the star don't realise is that a beautiful public park stretches out at the top of the bank. Originally these were the grounds of a privately-owned house, built in 1815 (the notice board has the wrong date) by the Rev. Walter M. Goalen, the uncle of William Gladstone (see p. 83), British prime minister in the late 1800s who visited Starbank as a child.

When Goalen died in 1889, the house and gardens were bought by Leith town council. The house was first used as a museum, then as a retirement club, and finally split into two tied houses for parks department employees to live in. In its time, the park has been a film star too: Clare Grogan and Tam White can be seen pushing a pram round it in the 1990 BBC Play on One, *The Wreck on the Highway*.

Eventually the council stopped paying for the upkeep of the garden and so it went into decline. In 2013 local resident Alastair Robertson was so dismayed at the state of it that he wrote to complain. He was persuaded by his local councillor to set up a Friends of the Park organisation: members meet on Wednesday and Saturday mornings to get stuck into gardening (anyone can join in). Kept true to the original formal Victorian layout, the park has symmetrical paths round beds of roses with a great sycamore tree at the centre. The Friends persuaded Forth Ports to donate redundant rowing boats, which now serve as nautically-themed planters.

The park is a perfect place to sit and view passing ships on the Forth – especially during the autumn, when sunsets are spectacular. And if you wait a while longer, you might see the navigational stars come out in the night sky above.

NEARBY

Next door, but closed to the public, is Strathavon Lodge, which was the home of James Young Simpson, who discovered the anaesthetic properties of chloroform. In front of the house is a statue of his dog, the recipient of many a chloroform experiment, and a bench where his friend Hans Christian Andersen used to sit – he called the area his "little Devon".

WEE MUSEUM OF NEWHAVEN

Victoria Primary School, Newhaven Main Street, Edinburgh EH6 4HY
• Tel: 0131 476 7306
• Open term time during school hours by appointment: please phone to book
• Admission free
• Buses: 11, 16

Shipshape ships

The Newhaven Heritage Museum used to be down the side of the harbour before Forth Ports jettisoned it to make room for an upscale restaurant strip. It was given a home by the nearby Victoria Primary School, which didn't have enough room to display the entire collection. However, each new term the pupils work with the local community to curate the contents and fill their school's reception rooms with objects and images documenting the area's rich past of fishing, oyster dredging and ship-building.

If you're familiar with Hill and Adamson's early black and white photographs of Newhaven fishwives, it's surprising to see a full-colour outfit on display, gaudily pinstriped in yellow, blue and pink. A wooden jigsaw shows how the local shoreline has changed over the past century as land has been reclaimed from the sea. But top of the class has to be the extraordinary model ships made by local welder and hobbyist George Scammell. He was particularly obsessed by the Scottish fleet of the fourteenth and fifteenth centuries, recreating each one of the thirty-odd galleons in painted wood, complete with hand-furled sails and knotted string rigging.

James IV's fleet, built in what was a kind of floating arms race with Europe, included what was to be the world's largest ship: the *Great Michael*, for which a new shipyard was created here at Newhaven, where the water was deeper than in Leith. Practically every oak tree in Fife was used in her building, and the reason why Craig Hall Road is so wide was to allow for their trunks to be brought down the hill horizontally.

Model boat-making also requires a surprising amount of wood and George was always persuading pals to help him chop up and carry chunks of pier timbers he'd reclaimed from the nearby coastal paths. His son Harry says his earliest memory is climbing over a lump of wood to get to his bed as his father's obsession with model-building took over their lives. Each boat took a couple of years to build, and George made two models of the *Great Michael* – the one now on display in Ocean Terminal was so big that the front door had to be taken off its hinges to get the ship out. Towards the end of his life, George became interested in Viking and Egyptian funeral boats, one of which can be found in another corner of this wee museum, as is a photograph of its creator, happily chiselling away at a block of wood.

WALL OF ADVANCED ROOFING ❻

Corner of Newhaven and Stanley Roads, Edinburgh EH6 4SJ
• Viewable 24 hours
• Free
• Buses: 7, 11

King's conundrum

A friend's daughter was walking back from Victoria Primary School, up the Newhaven Road, when she spotted a tiny king's head poking out from the side wall of Advanced Roofing: it was high up above her own head, about level with the Newhaven Road street sign, intricately detailed and wearing a medieval, perhaps Arthurian-style hooded crown. She was thrilled to find it. It really is tiny, maybe the size of a carved chess piece, made of a sort of tarnished pewter. What was it and why is it there?

Closer inspection reveals the wall to be full of treasures – a stone thistle, a lump of marble embossed with the letters ZZA, a rose-topped triangle inscribed with the date 1593. The edges of two of the little windows are lined with pebbles. The cement around the larger window is pargeted with a tile-like pattern and a handwritten date (1970) below a hammer and chisel, with a large snaking S on either side. What could they all mean?

The secretary at Advanced Roofing didn't know anything about it. But a neighbour across the road remembered Stanley Sutherland, who set up his building company there. He was quite a character and built the wall himself, filling it with bits of interesting masonry he'd picked up over the years, like a magpie feathering its nest with trinkets, or a Leith-based Gaudí decorating his walls with random broken objects. Where he found them nobody knows …

NEARBY

GREEN LANTERN

Three streets away, outside No. 17 York Road, is a strangely elaborate lamp post. Unlike the rest of the familiar olivey-brown tubular posts, this one is painted bright forest green with gold edging and a large hanging glass lantern. It is called a Bailie's lamp as one was installed outside the house of any Bailie (senior councillor) so that he could be quickly found in an emergency. A Provost (the Scots equivalent of a Mayor) had two of them, one for life and one removed on leaving office. This one is outside the house of Kenneth W. Borthwick, Lord Provost of Edinburgh from 1977 to 1980.

NEWHAVEN STATION

Newhaven Business Station, 85 Craighall Road, Edinburgh EH6 4RR
- Tel: 0131 554 4257
- www.newhavenstation.com
- Email: info@newhavenstation.com
- Admission free
- Tours by appointment and on Doors Open Day
- Buses: 7, 11

Station
to station

One of the themes of Irvine Welsh's novel *Trainspotting* is that the loss of the old rail lines to the north of Edinburgh – Leith, Newhaven, Granton, Pilton – took away a whole infrastructure. This resulted in the area's gradual exclusion and depression, with unemployment leading to a rise in drug use. There were no longer any trains to be spotted in Leith Central Station: it had become a derelict shell used by junkies as a shooting gallery.

Though this is a great metaphor for deindustrialisation, interestingly it was when the 1940s housing estates were built closer to the sources of employment – like the Granton Gas Works and the Madelvic car factory – that there was a drop in the use of trains from the city centre. Now employees either walked or took buses, and soon the rail lines couldn't turn a profit.

Those railway paths are now cycle lanes, with a few of the old stations still standing along their sides. The most beautifully restored is Newhaven Station, the only survivor of the five Caledonian Railway stations that ran between Caley Station on Princes Street and North Leith. Built in 1879, Newhaven was the penultimate stop on the Caledonian line. The last train departed on 28 April 1962.

Restored by retired fireman Richard Arnott, Newhaven is now a modern office space but with the fittings and fixtures of the old station and its original sign in bright blue. Built on wooden stilts, almost all of which needed replacing, the Haymarket/Ocean Terminal cycle path passes directly underneath it. You can visit the station on Doors Open Day, or even hire a hot desk space and become a "platformer" – the old building still supports businesses, but nowadays only those that transport their goods via wifi.

NEARBY

TRINITY STATION
North end of Trinity path; nearest postcode EH5 3LB
Viewable from outside only

Another old train station, which is now a private house, is about a 3 minutes' cycle or 20 minutes' walk from Newhaven Station at the end of the Trinity path. Just before you emerge onto Trinity Road is a double cottage on a high stone kerb with a white wooden fringed awning along the roof. The kerb used to be the train platform and the fringed cottage was Trinity Station, built especially for the fishwives to transport their fish up to town to sell. There were separate carriages for them; you can still see the small hatch (bottom right of the right-hand bay window) so that they could buy their tickets without entering the building with their pungent creels.

GRANTON GAS WORKS STATION
Waterfront Broadway, Edinburgh EH5 1SA
Viewable from outside only

The grandest of the remaining train stations is out near the old gas tower next to the giant new Morrison's. This huge red- and yellow-brick building was Granton Gas Works Station, which opened in 1903 especially for the gas workers. The arched window below the clock was where the walkway to the site was situated. You can see amazing pictures of the workers all crowded onto the platform in their three-piece suits on train expert Kenneth G Williamson's flickr site in the Edinburgh, Granton & Leith Railways album.

LIVING MEMORY ASSOCIATION

Ocean Terminal, Ocean Drive, Leith, Edinburgh EH6 6JJ
• www.livingmemory.org.uk
• Admission free
• Buses: 11, 21, 22, 34, 35, 36

Collecting recollections

The Ocean Terminal Shopping Centre opened in 2001 to much excitement: The List held its festival party there, everyone wanted to dine in the Conran Zinc Bar and sip Corporate Cosmopolitans as they gazed over the Forth. But it didn't take long for its shine to wear off, shoppers lured away to the next state-of-the-art designer centre, exposing the vast retail space as a rather soulless consumer experience.

But then a new heart started beating in one of the vacated units. The Living Memory Association, which originated just down the road in Quayside Street, was given a space. And this little non-profit organisation, with no design budget, business strategy or PR department, has transformed its unit into a genuinely moving experience.

The LMA collects something money can't buy: memories. Some of them oral, through recordings of stories and interviews; some of them archival, via online cataloguing of newspapers and photographs. But the space in Ocean Terminal is made of solid objects. Like a cross between a junk yard and a hoarder's living room, the LMA invites passing shoppers to come in, have a cup of tea and browse the collection. A 1951 EKCO television, a fading tin of Meggezones, a 1970s *Doctor Who* annual … Exhausted parents can have a seat on the sofa and flick through the photo albums, while kids can run around and examine vintage curiosities like a mechanical typewriter, bash a few keys and ask their grandparents, "Where's the screen?"

The brilliance of the LMA is that it bridges the gap between the generations. The objects simultaneously prompt older people's reminiscences and provoke children's curiosity. Unlike a museum collection, the objects are not precious: they can be handled, leafed through. Parents who warn their kids to put something down are reassured by the staff that it's okay, they can touch it! The collection is forever growing and transforming as visitors are moved to donate their own belongings: apparently useless objects which they've resisted throwing out for decades finally have a home and a value.

You can support the LMA by buying its publications like the perfectly named magazine, *TheLMA*. The association's tenancy at Ocean Terminal is insecure, however, so you might want to get there before the centre opts for another make-over. But hopefully the owners realise that the LMA is what has brought this terminal location back to life.

VINE TRUST BARGE

Prince of Wales Dock, Edinburgh EH6 7DX
- Tel: 0131 555 5598
- www.vinetrust.org
- Email: admin@vinetrust.org
- Visitable by appointment and on Doors Open Day
- Admission free
- Buses: 11, 16, 22, 35, 36

Water-based solution

L eith Docks are some of the oldest in Britain – archaeologists have found remnants of wharves here dating back as far as the 11th century. But moored in their basin is an unusual piece of modern architecture. Walk down through the gates at the foot of the Shore and keep on going: when you reach the roundabout at the bottom of Tower Place, you can see the Vine Trust Barge berthed at the dock in front of you.

The Vine Trust are an international volunteering charity who have set up medical ships in Peru on the Amazon river, and in Tanzania on Lake Victoria, providing free health and dental care to remote communities living near the water. Their operations used to be based out in East Lothian and really needed to be more centrally located, but the charity couldn't justify paying city-centre rents.

With all their nautical connections, the Trust discovered that the Ministry of Defence had an old decommissioned fuel barge floating around, and managed to persuade them to donate it to their cause. They talked the Forth

Ports into giving them a free mooring and secured the support of Archial Architects, who remodelled the boat as a shipshape office and teaching space, free of charge. Soon they had a new floating city headquarters, which won a Glasgow Institute of Architects Design Award.

Above deck is a beautiful long red cedar slatted glass room, taking full advantage of the location's panoramic views and the natural light glinting off the water. Below deck is a board/meeting room and a small 20-seater cinema where presentations can be screened. Or you could hire it for your own programme – perhaps a romantic barge-based triple bill: *Young Adam*, then *L'Atalante*, topped off with a dramatic finale, *The Bargee*?

CITADEL GARDEN

40/41 Commercial Street, Leith, Edinburgh EH6 6JD
• Viewable from behind rails 24 hours. Email jwdenholm@icloud.com to
arrange entry by appointment
• Admission free (though a small donation would be appreciated)
• Buses: 16, 22, 35, 36

**The
defence
rests**

I f you head to the side of the Tiso car
park in Leith, you will find an old stone
archway sitting incongruously beside the
brick-built outdoor warehouse and the line
of the sharp galvanised fence defending what
was once the railway line. A metal grille stops you walking through the arch,
but circle back past the Citadel Centre and up Dock Street: you can see the
other side of the archway and a pretty little fenced-off garden, with a bench
and flower pots among the pattern of cobbles and stone steps. What you are
actually looking at was once the eastern entrance to a vast pentagonal military
hub, stretching out along to Coburg Street, as far as Couper Street, and on the
other side along Commercial Street to Cromwell Place, that last name being a
clue as to its origins.

Oliver Cromwell had just executed Charles I and formed a commonwealth
when the Royalist Scots went and instated Charles II as king. It took Cromwell
months to break them, but finally the Scots made the schoolboy error of
actually coming out from behind their defences and were promptly decimated
by Cromwell's army. Leith was occupied and Cromwell's officer, General
Monck, housed all his weaponry and horses in whatever secure buildings he
could find – including the vaults of Trinity House (see p. 125). Feeling it wasn't
safe enough, he suggested building a fortified wall right around Leith. But
Edinburgh Town Council, spotting the potential for future misuse, dissuaded
him. And at great expense, part funded the building of a citadel instead.

But by the time it was completed in 1656, the conflict had died down. The
Citadel never got used for its original purposes and was mainly demolished
after only four years. Instead the area became a centre for industry, with
glass-making factories and the printing press of the *Mercurius Caledonius*
newspaper.

The stairs on the Dock Street side used to ascend to a house which sat on
top of the arch, photographs of which can be found online – or if you ask in
Tiso they might show you their copy. The area is actually the garden belonging
to the flats inside the Citadel Centre and if you email, they might kindly give
you a wee tour – climb onto the top of the arch, peer into the small dungeon
under the stairs and speculate as to what is bricked up in the hidden room
without doors …

VIM STONE

Front garden of Leith School of Art, 25 North Junction Street, Edinburgh
EH6 6HW
- Tel: 0131 554 5761
- Buses: 7, 10, 14, 21, 16, 22, 34, 35, 36

> **The stone
> that rocked
> a boat**

I n 1937 a ship named the *Vim* was sailing
from Norway to Edinburgh carrying a
boatload of timber when it ran aground
and started to let in perilous water. Luckily a
chunk of boulder broke off and plugged the
hole, preventing the vessel from sinking. The
ship and all its crew made it safely to Leith, whereupon they pulled the stone
out of the hull and carried it to the communion table of Leith's Norwegian
Seamen's Mission, offering thanks for their miraculous escape.

Now the Vim Stone is lodged in the front garden of the church, which has
since been transformed into an art school. It's difficult to spot the stone even
when you know it's there, but look for the three silver birch trees with their
silvery bark, planted behind as a symbol of the three guardian angels. An
embedded copper plaque bears a rhyming couplet inscription: "*Denne sten fra
norges bunn, bragte 'Vim' som gikk pa grunn*", which means "This stone, from
the bottom of Norway, brought 'Vim', which ran aground."

The church behind is also worth exploring as it was the first Norwegian
Seamen's Church, built in 1868. The Norwegian Seamen's Mission, founded
by Storjohann, wanted a church to serve Edinburgh's growing Scandinavian
community, especially the seafarers who faced such danger in their working
lives. The original design was by Danish architect Johan Schroder, but it was
adapted by Scottish architect James Simpson, giving the Scandinavian style a
Scottish spin. The most Scandinavian feature is the tall narrow spire with fish-
scale tiles; the rest of the building is made of more hefty Scottish stone, though
its roof has a Scandinavian steepness designed to discourage deep snow from
gathering.

NORWEGIANS IN EDINBURGH

There is still a large Norwegian population in Edinburgh, some originating
from the shipping business, while many others escaped here during the
Second World War when their homeland was occupied. On 17 May every
year, Edinburgh hosts the largest Norwegian Independence Day parade
outside Oslo. The cultures are not so distant: plenty of Scots words derive
from Old Norse – words like bairn, midden, muckle and even kilt (from the
verb *kjalta*, to fold). Norway also has oil, tartan and a penchant for dark
detective stories, not to mention a certain proclivity for hard spirits. So
raise a glass to the Norse gods who sent a stone to plug a hole and brought
those sailors safe to our shores.

DAVID WILKINSON MURALS

Lane between Bernard Street and Carpet Lane, Leith, Edinburgh EH6 6SP
• Buses: 22, 35, 36
& Bonnington Road, Edinburgh EH6 5JB
• Buses: 7, 10, 14, 21, 24, 36
• Viewable 24 hrs
• Admission free

Glass thrice full

Leith's most famous mural can be seen on the gable end of the library on North Junction Street. It was painted by Tim Chalk and Paul Grime, and in 2014 was listed in *The Guardian*'s top ten murals of the world.

Together with artist David Wilkinson, Chalk and Grime had set up Artists Collective, which obtained a grant for a project to fill the then depressed streets of Leith with art. If you look in the right places, you will find some slightly shyer, more clandestine murals, which Wilkinson created solo.

Venture up the wee gunnel leading through from Bernard Street to Carpet Lane (see overleaf) and you'll find Wilkinson's playful *trompe-l'œil* mural of a Leith trader heaving a tea chest out of a doorway in the stone wall. On a small blue painted plaque (top right) is the name of the piece, *Carpet Lane Traders*, above credits for the SDA funders (Scottish Development Agency), the Leith Project and a dated copyright symbol: DWA–David Wilkinson Art. Below is the telephone number 552 0295, which, if you hoped to get through and speak to the artist or place an order of tea, is sadly unattainable.

Another of Wilkinson's wonderful murals is high up on the back gable end of the building where Bonnington Road meets Great Junction Street. Here the artist has created a huge *trompe-l'œil* arched window, with different local industries reflected in it – flour milling and breadmaking. The huge Swanfield Flour Mill used to stand opposite here; the last remaining part of it is the building at No. 26. In Wilkinson's painted glass, you will find three layers of images – first, figures engraved into the glass: a farmer harvesting wheat, a miller grinding flour, a baker kneading dough; second, the view reflected by its surface: local buildings and a church spire; and, lastly, decorations painted onto the glass itself: wheat kernels and sheaves, millstones, foxes, poppies and cornflowers.

The lowest section has disintegrated as it was painted on puttied cement but it featured a beautifully simple montage of the machinery involved from farm to factory: tractors ploughing fields, a combine harvester, a delivery lorry. All around the edges is painted stonework, blending with the brickwork of the actual building. The entire piece is so clever and so fascinating that every time you pass it in the car, for once you wish the traffic lights at the junction would stay on red.

EVOLUTION OF LEITH SCULPTURES

Carpet Lane, Leith, Edinburgh EH6 6SE
• Open 24 hrs
• Admission free
• Buses: 16, 22, 35, 36

> *Swept under the carpet*

Where Carpet Lane meets Maritime Street, there is a thicket of undergrowth and unruly trees sprouting from a raised walled bed. Pleasant as the foliage may be, it is actually obscuring a far more interesting piece of art which you really have to be chasing squirrels or taking your hedge diving pretty seriously to spot. Along the back wall are a series of twelve sculptures called the *Evolution of Leith*. They were created by artist brothers Kenny and Gordon Munro as part of the 1987 Leith Project, which aimed to bring a bit of creative enhancement to gap sites in the as yet un-gentrified Leith.

The sculptures are made from flat square sheets of galvanised steel onto which the artists chalked the designs, cut them out with an oxyacetylene torch and then bent them so that they stood in relief, like pages from a giant's pop-up book. The series moves from left to right, starting with vine leaves, a design taken from the top of a nearby building, suggesting an organic or a Roman origin. As you move, or rather scrabble, to your right, you see the evolving industries of Leith: fishing, ship-building, and eventually wine bars and nouvelle cuisine, a scene which was starting to emerge in the 1980s.

Kenny and Gordon were brought into the project by the artist David Wilkinson, whose wonderful mural is just round the corner (see previous page). This was the first time the brothers had collaborated on an art project. They have since worked together on a piece in Braehead, near Glasgow. Theirs is a pretty artistic family: Dad Jim was a jazz musician, artist and Edinburgh College of Art lecturer, whose stainless-steel sculpture *Quartet* now stands inside the Scottish Parliament.

NEARBY

On the corner at the other end of Carpet Lane is Catchpell House (EH6 6SP). Above the doorway is a painting of people who seem to be simply hanging around a courtyard in their knickerbockers. They are in fact playing catchpell, as this was once the site of a catchpell court – the Scots version of Royal or "Real" Tennis. The name derives from *caich pule*, old Scots/Flemish for "a game of chases". Often called the sport of kings as it was favoured by the royals, this was an indoor tennis game played in a walled court, like a cross between tennis and squash. The oldest surviving court is over the water in Falkland Palace, Fife, and dates back to 1539.

LEITH POLICE STATION JAIL

79 Constitution Street, Edinburgh EH6 7EY
• Access: rarely, via appointment and only with security clearance
• Contact: EdinburghLeithWalkCPT@scotland.pnn.police.uk
• Sometimes on Doors Open Day (late Sept)
• Buses: 12, 16

Cell Division

Looking at the classical, pillared two-storey façade of 79 Constitution Street, you'd never guess there was a jail inside. The clue is to look closely at the top row of three sash windows. See how the frames slope inwards towards the top? Means they're non-operational. And those Venetian blind slats you can see behind? Yep, dummy ones cast out of concrete. That's because on the other side of this elegant bit of architecture is a line of four prison cells, which do not afford a pleasant view. They form the top row of a block of sixteen cells which have been there since 1833 and were in use right up until 2003. Until then, they were the oldest operational cell block in the country.

Originally the cells mainly held prisoners awaiting trial in the court room down the corridor next door. Prisoners could be driven in through the archway below and dispatched to the cells internally. The Victorians were very keen on hygiene, so prisoners were stripped naked, doused in caustic soda powder and hosed down before being dressed in sackcloth and dispatched lice-free to their personal accommodation.

Each cell is about the width of a man's outstretched arms and just long enough to lie down in. They had luxury flushing toilets, with little wooden buttock warmers, the cisterns being out of reach on the outside of the cell. The cell doors are thick and have a rather loftily placed spy hole, designed at a time when officers had to be a minimum height of 5 foot 10 (1.788 metres), so many post-1990 recruits had to stand on tippy toes to check on their residents. This is one reason why the cells failed to meet new health and safety regulations in 2003. Plus, the doors were rather inadequately secured by a simple hasp and padlock. The staircase was another hazard: stairs are a dangerous place to deal with a prisoner who is resisting being moved. Especially when the treads have been worn away by the officers' hobnail boots.

Now the cells are used to lock away case documents instead of criminals, and only one can be entered. But if you are lucky and patient in arranging an appointment, the Leith Police just might let you do a bit of time in there.

NEARBY

In 1823 the last two men executed for piracy in Scotland were hanged at the north end of Constitution Street. Frenchman François Gautiez and his Swedish cohort Peter Heaman were found guilty of capturing the brig *Jane*, killing the captain, smoking out the rest of the crew by locking them in the hold with smoke bombs, and stealing eight barrels of silver. Tens of thousands of folk turned out to watch them be hanged over water, the traditional method of pirate dispatch.

OLD LEITH TOWN HALL

Leith Police Station, 81 Constitution Street, Edinburgh EH6 6AF
• Access: rarely, via appointment and only with security clearance
• Contact: EdinburghLeithWalkCPT@scotland.pnn.police.uk
• Sometimes open on Doors Open Day (late Sept)
• Buses: 12, 16

*A court
in waiting*

The reception area of Leith Police Station is just like any other police station you've ever had the pleasure to visit: a small room unadorned save the various flyers and warning notices, a couple of desks protected by thick glass, and a couple of plastic moulded waiting chairs. But if you're lucky enough to be escorted through the security doors, what a treat lies in store …

The station is housed in a grand edifice which was built by R&R Dickson in 1827 as Leith's court house. In 1833 Leith became an independent borough and its councillors moved in. In 1868 they extended the building into the terrace next door, creating a town hall complex fitted out by James Simpson, Leith's town architect. In 1920 Leith was rather forcibly amalgamated into Greater Edinburgh and the council moved out.

Like a shore-based *Marie Celeste*, the City Chambers room stands just as it was when the council evacuated nearly a century ago. You get an inkling of its grandeur as you climb the wide marble staircase with its impressive stained-glass arched windows, featuring the Leith crest. Head through a 1905 crested archway and you will enter a dark and dusty but ridiculously ornate room: red leather chairs, elaborately extended gold door-handle mouldings, carved wooden dado panelling … Gold-framed paintings fill every wall with portraits of Leith provosts in all their finery, and half of one wall is taken up by Alexander Carse's grand depiction of *The Landing of George IV at Leith* (1822). Look up and you'll discover the wildly camp Thomas Bonnar-designed ceiling, its three ceiling roses bordered by layer upon layer of intricate interweaving leaf and flower patterns in dusky pink and mint green.

It seems bizarre that all of this finery surrounded the courts as they adjudicated over disputes such as an 1886 custody battle over a pony, a 1909 £2 betting dispute and, in 1920, two Swedes being in possession of Bolshevik pamphlets.

As the adjacent rooms are used for high-security operations, visitors are only allowed in on Doors Open Day, though in 2012, 450 schoolkids were invited to take part in a mock trial there: this time the case involved the theft of a mobile phone. Probably worth less than one of the doorknobs round here.

TRINITY HOUSE

TRINITY HOUSE

99 Kirkgate, Leith, Edinburgh EH6 6BJ
• www.trinityhouseleith.org.uk
• Open Mon–Fri. Free admission; donations welcome
• Tours by appointment: call 0131 554 3289 five days in advance to arrange
• Buses: 1, 7, 10, 12, 14, 16, 22, 25, 35, 49

Hidden treasure house

Trinity House is one of those museums which isn't on people's radar because it's hidden in the back streets of Leith, landlocked by the Newkirkgate Shopping Centre and South Leith parish church. Those who accidentally stumble across it as they park at the back of Farmfoods don't pop in for a visit because you have to book a week in advance. But please get organised and book your passage aboard: inside this perfectly preserved Georgian neoclassical house is the headquarters of the Master Mariners of Leith and an absolutely fascinating collection of all things nautical.

On the ground floor there's the beautifully appointed Masters' meeting room with its fireplace commemorating the battle of Camperdown, perched on top of which is a small penguin carved from a whale's tooth. In the hall there's a fully working antique toilet. At the foot of the stairs is an intriguing tropical seed ballot box with a funnel into which you insert your hand and discreetly drop your seed into the "yes" or "no" chamber. On the double stairway is an impressive stained-glass window commemorating the merchant seamen who lost their lives in the Great War.

But it's the room upstairs which will really float your boat. The grand Convening Room is filled with a 6-metre-long table, every part of it strewn with maritime memorabilia and nautical knick-knacks, all kinds of navigation and measuring devices (sextants, octants, compasses, barometers), long leather sail-menders' thimbles, a toothy sawfish blade, the wing of a flying fish and a 3-metre-long narwhal tusk, which this strange whale/unicorn uses as a highly sensitive measuring probe.

All around the room are miniature models of famous ships. Look up and you'll see an ornate coral, turquoise and gold plaster ceiling featuring Neptune, dolphins and lots of knotted ropes. On the walls are not one but four original portraits by Henry Raeburn. On one mantelpiece, a strange white gnarly lump the size of a coconut turns out to be the eardrum of a 200-year-old whale.

You can also visit the vaults, which were part of the original almshouse built by the Trinity in 1555. When Oliver Cromwell's army invaded and seized the house in 1650, they used this as a store.

MUSEUM OF BOXING

Upstairs at the Leith Victoria Amateur Athletic Club
28 Academy Street, Leith, Edinburgh EH6 7EF
• Admission free, by appointment: 0131 333 1112
• Email: info@leith-victoria-aac.com
• Buses: 21, 25, 34, 35, 49

*Above
the ropes*

In 2011 Leith Victoria Athletic's club secretary, Douglas Fraser, received a call from Ian Mackintosh, a volunteer at the Grangemouth Heritage Trust. He had found an Amateur Boxing Association 1921 silver trophy cup in their collection, inscribed with the name "Alex Ireland", who had been one of LVAAC's boxers. When the Trust donated the trophy back to the club, ex-boxer, coach and Olympic referee Fraser realised he had loads of medals, trophies and boxing memorabilia scattered around, and it was high time he did something with it.

Four years later, after a bit of a brush-up – one solid silver cup was completely black after being used as an ashtray by the jannies (caretakers) –, a little boxing museum opened above the Bell Gymnasium, on the edge of Leith Links. It's the UK's first museum devoted to boxing and, despite being small, it punches well above its weight. Leith Victoria Athletic is not only Scotland's oldest boxing club, it's one of the highest-achieving in the UK – on the wall is a list of over 120 titles won by the members, and that's only the ones that the club knows about. They can boast two world champions, three Olympic and five Commonwealth Games Medallists. The museum's cases are crammed with silverware, memorabilia and photographs of boxing legends who came out of the club – Tancy Lee, first winner of the Lonsdale Belt in 1919, the year when the club started; Alex Arthur, who held World and European super-featherweight and gold in the 1998 Commonwealth Games; Steven Simmons, three times Scottish Champion. The club itself is the first amateur club to be inducted into Scotland's Hall of Fame, an honour usually only given to individual boxers.

But some of the best exhibits are the more humble ones – the ex-army hut shed down by the Victoria shipyard, where the club first started. Lee Sharp's membership card from when he was a rather podgy kid, next to a picture of him a decade later rippling with muscle. Wonderful photographs of Tancy Lee posing in 1920s polo neck and high-waisted tights. The four Bell brothers (after whom the Gymnasium is named), towering in slick '50s suits beside their proud mum.

The museum is not only a fascinating glimpse into the club's history, it's also a huge inspiration to the young boxers coming up through the club now. And with a few female boxers joining the gym, maybe one day there'll be a woman's name up on that wall.

> The golden boy on top of the dome of the Old Quad, sculpted by John Hutchison in 1888, is a 6-foot-high bronze figure modelled on an Edinburgh boxer, Anthony Hall.

HINDU MANDIR AND CULTURAL CENTRE

St Andrew Place, Leith, Edinburgh EH6 7EG
• Tel: 0789 0726 117
• www.edinburghhindumandir.org.uk
• Email: info@edinburghhindumandir.org.uk
• Open to the public Mon–Sat 9.30am–11.30am and 6pm–8pm, Sun 11am–2pm. Admission free

The body of a temple

The Hindu Mandir on the edge of Leith Links is rather more sober-looking than the average Indian temple. No shining marble edifice covered in intricate carvings of deities, this is a grand but austere grey windowless neoclassical stone building with four imposing pillars supporting a simple portico, the only concession to adornment being bookish scrolls at the pillar tops.

Constructed in 1827 as St Andrew's United Associate Church, the building changed hands several times over the years, but remained Scottish Presbyterian of one flavour or another. It finally fell vacant in 1983, and for the next six years, slowly crumbling, it stoically awaited its next master. When the Edinburgh Hindu community purchased it, it was in a bad way. Raising the funds to restore a derelict building was hard, but the community persevered, and in 2011 the building reopened both as a place of worship and as a space for traditional Hindu arts such as music, language, dance and yoga.

So now, the dark, solemn interior is filled with colour, sound and light. The ground floor is a community arts space, the first floor a temple. On Sundays and festivals, the floor by the foot of the grand stairwell is knee-deep in discarded shoes. Add yours to the pile and climb the stairs and you will enter a bright room filled with worshippers sitting cross-legged on the white carpet, listening to the priest. He also sits on the ground, surrounded by musicians who give his words musical punctuation with *tabla* drums and *manjira* cymbals.

Down one side of the room, watching from behind a golden arched shrine, are shining white marble sculptures of the Hindu deities, carved and hand painted in Jaipur. Each is dressed in matching opulent robes, changed for the different festivals. At their feet are offerings of Indian sweets, fruit and flowers.

GRETNA TRAIN CRASH MURAL

Drill Hall, 36 Dalmeny Street, Edinburgh EH6 8RG
- Viewable Mon–Sat 10am–5pm
- Admission free
- Buses: 1, 7, 10, 12, 14, 16, 22, 25, 35, 49

Gretna giant

Down the side of the Drill Hall in Leith is a wide outdoor passageway, where plants catch some sunlight and smokers grab a nicotine fix. The high brick wall is slicked in thick grey and white paint and it is not until you stand back from it that you see what it depicts. Staring out from the wall is the face of a man – his eyes are wrinkled and he is smiling. And yet this is a memorial to a terrible disaster which occurred over 100 years ago, on 22 May 1915: the Gretna rail crash, the worst train disaster in British railway history in which 227 people were killed and 246 injured. One hundred and two of those killed were young men from the 7th Leith Battalion of the Royal Scots, who had trained at the Drill Hall and were on their way to fight in Gallipoli (Turkey). The bodies of the victims were brought back and laid out in the Drill Hall for the families to identify, before being buried in Rosebank cemetery, on the other side of Leith Walk.

The mural was painted by Brisbane-born artist Guido van Helten, whose giant faces stare out from gable ends and hoardings across the world. He was in Glasgow, painting commissioned portraits of athletes on the sides of houses for the Commonwealth Games, when he contacted contemporary public art organisation LeithLate. He hoped they could find him a space to do a more personal piece – his own work rather than a corporate commission – while he was still in Scotland. LeithLate introduced him to the Drill Hall and the arts development organisation Out of the Blue, which is based there.

Van Helten likes to refer to the locality in his work, and having heard about the Gretna rail crash, he felt moved to respond. He found an archive photograph of one of the few survivors, who had lived into old age, with only his initials to suggest who he was. With the photo displayed on his iphone, van Helten took spray cans and worked freehand, no stencils, no pencil outlines, no dust sheets to prevent spray drift – and completed the piece in only two days. It was initially launched as part of the Forest Fringe festival in 2014 and then became the centrepiece of Gretna 100 – the May 2015 events commemorating the centenary of the disaster.

LEITH WALK POLICE BOX

Croall Place, Leith Walk, Edinburgh EH7 4LT
• www.leithwalkpolicebox.com
• www.edinburghexpoliceboxes.co.uk
• Opening hours and admissions vary
• Buses: 7, 10, 11, 12, 14, 16, 22, 25, 49

Boxes of delight

Edinburgh's police boxes are something totally unique to the city. Other cities dismantled most of their concrete and timber structures in the 1980s, once radio and mobile phones meant they'd outlived their policing use. But Edinburgh's were made of cast iron and proved practically indestructible: they had been forged in the Carron Foundry near Falkirk (which also made cannons) after a design by Ebenezer James MacRae, Edinburgh City Architect in the 1930s. Complementing the city's classical architecture, the boxes had pillared and panelled façades, saltire-patterned windows, Edinburgh crest mouldings and a neoclassical sloped roof, topped off with a flashing light to alert bobbies to emergency calls.

Inside was a telephone, a desk, a fold-down seat, pigeon holes for filing, and a sink that apparently doubled as a toilet … though its design rather failed to predict the advent of the WPC. The boxes were mini police stations, sometimes used as temporary holding cells. There are also tales of swans being detained, of policemen kipping out in them after a big night, and of the box over the public toilets on Albert Street being used to stake out the cottaging scene below.

Of the 140 original boxes, 85 survive. In the early 1990s, a first batch was auctioned off and bought up mainly for use as coffee stalls and snack food booths – like "Bollywood: The Coffee Box" at Bruntsfield Place, or the Brazilian food kiosk "Tupiniquim" on Lauriston Place. But then people started coming up with more diverse uses for them. Biologist Monty Roy bought her Leith Walk one in 2012 for just short of £10,000. She was thrilled to have won the auction, though restoring the peeling, grafittied, moss- and pigeon-guano-covered 2-tonne lump of rusting iron required much loving labour.

Roy decided to use hers as a pop-up community space and started inviting people to pitch ideas for it, with lets as short as 4 hours. So far, it has been used as an art gallery, a school kids' project museum, a referendum campaign hub and a community tool library. In July 2015 Roy's was one of ten police boxes to take part in the Edinburgh Police Box Festival, where they formed a network of venues for performances, storytelling, comedy, theatre and art displays. It was such a success that an annual event is now planned, so check Roy's website for details.

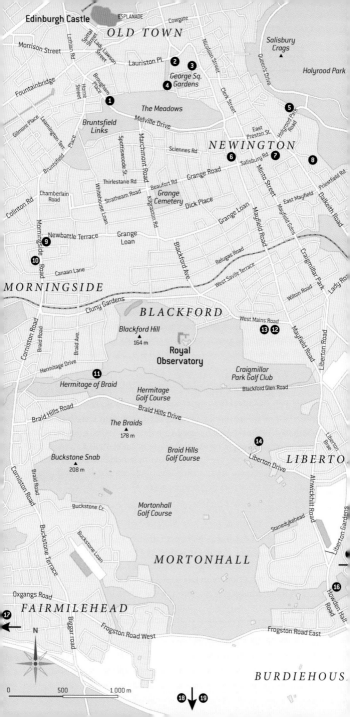

SOUTH

MEMORIAL MASONS' PILLARS

The Meadows, Brougham Place, Edinburgh EH3 9HW
• Viewable 24 hrs. Admission free
• Bus: 24

Quarry Man

As you enter the Meadows from the Tollcross end of Melville Drive, you will pass two 8-metre-high octagonal stone pillars on either side of the road, slightly hidden in the trees. These are the Memorial Masons' Pillars, designed by Sir James Gowans to mark the 1886 Great Exhibition (see overleaf for more), of which he was chairman.

The pillars, which were built by the Master Builders and Operative Masons of Edinburgh and Leith, were initially in a much more prominent position – right on the corners of Lonsdale Terrace –, but in the 1970s they were moved back from the road edge. Now they are dwarfed by lime trees which, at the time of construction, would have been mere saplings shaded by the octagonal trunk of these twin pillars.

Gowans was quite a maverick and was clearly obsessed with stone. He lived in the peculiar gothic pagoda called "Rockville", which he had built on Napier Road for his second wife – the first having died in a mysterious bath accident. Sadly demolished in the sixties, only the distinctive gate piers remain, but it originally had a five-storey, oriental-style tower and was chequered by the use of stone from all the different quarries of Scotland.

Gowans went for the same rock theme with the Memorial Masons' Pillars, which are banded because they are made up of eighteen different types of specimen stone, each inscribed with their quarry name. Places like Dunmore, Polmaise, Whitsome Newton. The idea was to compare how the different stones weathered. There were fourteen different finishes as well, with descriptions such as "nidged", "hammer-daubed", "fine-broached", "splitter-striped" and "stugged".

The caps and the central bands are carved with coats of arms and crests. On top of each one sits a red sandstone unicorn, adopted as the national animal of Scotland by King Robert in the late 1300s.

At the other end of Melville Drive are two more pillars, one topped by a unicorn, the other by a lion, but those were installed much earlier by publisher Thomas Nelson. He donated the columns in thanks for the city's generosity towards him when his printworks got burnt down by a terrible fire.

1886 INTERNATIONAL EXHIBITION OF INDUSTRY, SCIENCE AND ART

In the corner of the meadows nearest to the foot of Lauriston Gardens, you will find a sundial erected to commemorate Prince Albert Victor's opening of the International Exhibition of Industry, Science and Art. It is inscribed with lots of time-based aphorisms like, "Well-arranged time is the surest sign of a well-arranged mind" and "Time is the chrysalis of eternity".

Now imagine yourself travelling back through such time to 8 May 1886. Prince Albert Victor was cutting the ribbon to a vast event: the whole of this side of the meadows was filled with a gigantic ornate hall, a cross between Waverley Station and the Brighton Pavilion, with a palatial, zodiac-decorated domed entrance facing Brougham Place.

It was a World Expo in the style of the original one held in London in 1851, which had become quite *de rigueur* for the Victorians. Over the summer months, thousands flocked to see the latest in the arts and crafts, inventions and new technology. They boarded the electric railway that ran between Brougham Place and Middle Meadow Walk. They imagined bygone days as they wandered through reconstructions of 17th-century Edinburgh streets like the Netherbow Port and the Black Turnpike.

The gift-shop attendants were dressed in full 17th-century costume. Even the souvenirs were spectacular, like a carved ivory cross containing a tiny metal "Stanhoscope", through which you could see magnified micro-photographs of the exhibition.

The whole thing was so wonderful that people wanted it to stay for more than just the summer – and that had been the original intention – but sadly they had overlooked an act of parliament that forbade any permanent building on the Meadows. The fabulous edifice and all of its marvels closed to the public on 30 October 1886 and vanished into the mists of time, apart from the sundial, the Memorial Masons' Pillars (see previous page) and one or two other traces ... (see facing page).

TRACES OF THE GREAT EXHIBITION

Behind the Pavilion Café (Jawbone Walk, Melville Drive, EH9 1JU), you'll find the recently restored arch made of four whale's jawbones over the foot of Jawbone Walk. These were used as poles for the tepee that formed the Shetland and Fair Isle knitting stand, part of the Women's Industries display.

In Nicolson Square Gardens (EH8 9BH) stands the Brass Iron Founders' pillar, the exhibit of the Edinburgh and Leith Brass Founders. Each panel features a coat of arms of a Scottish burgh. Wielding his hammer at the top is Tubal-cain, the first brass worker, mentioned in the Bible.

At the Café Royal (19 West Register Street, EH2 2AA), notice the six framed Royal Doulton tile paintings that were originally shown at the exhibition. They feature inventors like Michael Faraday and James Watt at the very moment of discovery.

On top of Calton Hill, behind the Stewart Monument, look out for a Portuguese cannon decorated with the Royal Arms of Spain – plunder taken from the Burmese war and brought to Edinburgh for display at the exhibition.

ANATOMICAL MUSEUM ❷

University of Edinburgh
1st floor, Doorway 3, Medical School, Teviot Place, Edinburgh EH8 9AG
• www.ed.ac.uk/biomedical-sciences/anatomy
• Access: last Sat of each month. Closed June, July and Dec
• Entry free, but donations welcome
• Buses: 2, 23, 27, 35, 41, 42, 45, 47, 60, 67

The
anatomy
of research

It's pretty tricky to get your timings right for visiting the Anatomical Museum as it's only open on the last Saturday of each month, and not at all in June, July or December. But your forward planning will be thoroughly rewarded by a tour of the most dramatic display of 300 years of anatomical research. Back when the museum moved here in 1880, Edinburgh was the world centre of anatomical teaching, and those who studied these artefacts included Charles Darwin, Thomas Hodgkin, James Young Simpson and Arthur Conan Doyle.

The entrance to the museum alone is quite breathtaking – two towering elephant skeletons guard the doorway, a whale's jawbone nestles into a high arch and a 3D hologram morphs between the human organs, muscular

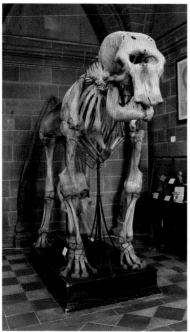

and nervous systems. The main floor is filled with skeletons, models and preserved prosections. The back wall is lined with white plaster head casts used for the study of phrenology, including that of Franz Joseph Gall, founder of this now outdated "science". Though some of the displays are not for the faint of heart, many pieces are unexpectedly beautiful, such as the coral-like resin casts of the lung's vessels.

Star residents include "Mercury Man" – a corpse preserved in lacquer who is the result of one of the earliest methods of studying the body's workings, by mercury injection, which would trace the route of whichever system it entered. Mercury Man may be shrivelled and blackened but he helped Alexander Monro II understand the lymphatic system.

Here too is the skeleton of the notorious William Burke, who is still carrying out his 1829 sentence: to be hanged, dissected and put on display in the museum, like those bodies he had so over-zealously supplied.

If you ask nicely, you can be taken up a winding back staircase to the artists' garret, where diagrams for teaching were produced. In the corner is a hoist to bring body parts up through a trapdoor from the dissection room below. And in the centre stands a specially built display table, with a hole for draining fluids.

It's worth organising yourself to get here soon as there are plans to move the museum alongside the Surgeons' Hall. This would have the advantage of allowing many more of the thousands of objects to come out from storage in the catacombs below Teviot, but the amazing sense of travel back to a time when this place was at the heart of the scientific world would be sadly lost.

You can donate your own body after death for anatomical examination, an act of selflessness for which the university would be extremely grateful. Search Anatomy@Edinburgh and, for further information, see their pages on "Donating your body".

DELIVERY HATCHES

In the postgraduate law lecture theatre in the Old College, off West College Street, you will see a trap-door entrance to a flight of stone steps. These go down to an underground passageway, which once led right down to the Cowgate and the vaults below the South Bridge (see p. 41). This was where bodies emerged from underground tunnels for discreet delivery to the medical school.

Until the 1832 Anatomy Act, only the corpses of executed murderers could be used for dissection, and hangings were few and far between. So with the study of anatomy being at such a pivotal stage, a market in the recently deceased sprang up. This started with grave robbing, as practised by the "Resurrectionists", and escalated to the more direct murder preferred by Burke and Hare: death by asphyxiation so as to minimise signs of violence was called "Burking".

Their main customer was the flamboyant surgeon Dr Robert Knox, who lived at 4 Newington Place, and had his practice in a building which stood near to Chisholm House in High School Yards, behind the Centre for Carbon Innovation. If you peer down into the basement beneath the stairs, you will see a rather suspicious-looking hatch in the wall. Though the popular rhyme ran "Burke's the butcher, Hare's the thief, Knox the boy who buys the beef!", only Burke was executed, while Hare escaped and the courts found Knox innocent. But the folk of Edinburgh disagreed with the verdict and an angry lynch mob came after Knox. He managed to escape, but was expelled from the Royal College of Surgeons and the Royal Society of Edinburgh and effectively banned from teaching in Scotland.

GEMS OF GEORGE SQUARE

Informatics Forum, 10 Crichton Street, Edinburgh EH8 9AB
Exhibition Gallery, Main Library, George Square, Edinburgh EH8 9LJ
• Tel: 0131 650 8379
• www.libraryblogs.is.ed.ac.uk
• Email: is-crc@ed.ac.uk
• Library opening times vary, usually 7.30am–2.30am
• Admission free
• Buses: 41, 42, 67

Nano memorials

George Square is full of all sorts of hidden art and interesting objects, easily missed due to their small size and the strewing of students over every available step or surface. On a sunny day, you might have to move one or two to find the Haynes Nano Stage outside the Informatics Forum on the corner of Crichton Street and Charles Street. Photos of it tend to be misleading scale-wise: what you're looking for is about the size of a coffee-table book. Because that's what it is – a book cast in stainless steel.

Sculptor David Forsyth wanted to allude to the way in which Jim Haynes' Paperback Bookshop, which stood here in the 1960s, had set the stage for many cultural activities. Haynes now lives in Paris, where he runs Sunday dinners from his home – literary socials open to anyone who emails and makes a contribution – but back in the 60s his bookshop was the centre of Edinburgh's own counter-culture beat scene. It famously had a real stuffed Indian rhino head sticking out of the front of the building, looking as if it had charged out of the bookshop and got trapped in the wall. If you peer round the corner towards Bristo Square, you'll find a much smaller bronze head by sculptor William Darrell, perched high up the wall, well out of petting reach.

Keep your eyes peeled as you walk around the edges of George Square and you'll find plaques to all sorts of interesting ex-students: writers Sir Walter Scott, Robert Louis Stevenson and Jane Welsh Carlyle; medical students like Benjamin Rush, who signed the American Declaration of Independence, and James Africanus Horton, Edinburgh's first African graduate and the first West African writer to call for independence; and economics and history graduate Julius Kambarage Nyerere, the first President of Tanzania.

If you wander through the garden in the centre of the square, you'll find a tiny hedged labyrinth to get lost in. Should you successfully re-find yourself, you can head over to the University Library, where there is a tiny museum in the entrance way, with changing displays from the University's Centre for Research Collections. On one visit you might find the Paolozzi miniature maquettes, another time a diminutive display on Dolly the sheep. There's more inside on the ground floor and up on the sixth floor, which non-students can view by signing in as visitors.

HIDDEN GARDEN CHAPEL OF ST ALBERT THE GREAT

St Albert's Catholic Chaplaincy, George Square Lane, Edinburgh EH8 9LD
(entrance off George Square Lane, opposite Peter's Yard café)
• Tel: 0131 650 0900
• www.scotland.op.org/edinburgh
• Open daily: 8am–6pm (outside Mass times). Admission free
• Buses: 23, 27, 35, 41, 42, 45, 47, 67

A translucent temple

As you stroll down Middle Meadow Walk, the chapel of St Albert the Great is only a short distance away. And yet it's almost invisible, its silhouette cleverly hidden by the wall at the back of George Square Lane.

Wander through the gate marked by the St Albert's Catholic Chaplaincy plaque and the chapel is revealed – a strikingly beautiful piece of modern architecture, fitting perfectly into its setting and yet in complete contrast to the high tenements behind it, which are in fact the remnants of Edinburgh's first Georgian square. A pale, thick stone wall forms one side of the chapel, and a wooden sail of a roof appears to float over it, held up, it seems, by four oxidised steel tree trunks. The gable is glass, making the whole chapel light and ethereal. This is like something you would find on the coast of Los Angeles, not in the heart of Old Edinburgh.

The inside is just as stunning: the walls are slatted wood, curving to form the ceiling and allowing light to shine through both from the side and overhead. We are so used to churches with no view and only the light from narrow stained-glass windows that it's quite a shock to be bathed in the stuff – especially if you visit in the afternoon.

As the garden is in a conservation area and has a great sycamore tree, Edinburgh Planning Department restricted the chapel to a much smaller space than had been hoped for. But the boundaries seem merely to have inspired greater creativity. The glass gable is almost invisible and the canopy extends beyond the walls and creates an illusion of space, reaching out into the garden without treading on the precious roots of the sycamore.

The simplicity of the style, the decorative restraint and the limited palette of materials is very much in keeping with the Dominican approach. Everything is beautifully hand-crafted and there are all sorts of clever practical features – for example, the pews can be shortened to allow more room for large ceremonies. The confession room is hidden behind an invisible door to the left of the entrance.

The architects Simpson & Brown collaborated closely with their Dominican community clients, who were well versed in architecture and so very hands on – in fact, not only did the building win many architectural awards from the likes of RIBA and the RIAS, but the Chaplaincy also won a Scottish Government/RIAS client award.

INNOCENT & SCOTLAND STREET TUNNELS

Innocent railway tunnel, next to East Parkside junction with Holyrood Park Road, Edinburgh EH16 5XN
• Open 24 hrs • Admission free
• Buses: 2, 14, 30, 33
Scotland Street tunnel entrance, viewable from Platform 19, Waverley Station, Edinburgh EH1 1BD
• Buses: 3, 14, 29, 30, 31, 33, 37, 49. Tram: St Andrew Square. Rail: Waverley Station

Double tunnel vision

There are two remarkable ex-railway tunnels running under the streets of central Edinburgh. One, the Innocent tunnel, is open to the public as a cycle path, and the other, the Scotland Street tunnel, is sealed off. Both were built by Victorian engineers about ten years apart, but with such steep inclines that they required a stationary engine to haul the trains up their tracks.

A narrow Victorian postbox marks the spot on Holyrood Park Road beneath which you will find the start of the Innocent tunnel, which is part of the old line between St Leonard's and Dalkeith. Built in 1829 by James Jardine, it was the first public railway tunnel in Scotland. It runs down a 1-in-30 incline for just over half a kilometre before emerging below Samson's Ribs on the edge of Holyrood Park. Originally for transporting coal, it soon allowed a passenger service, mainly for day-trippers to Portobello.

There are several theories as to how it got its name. Either because no fatal accidents occurred during its building. Or because it allowed so many request stops that nobody bothered to issue tickets. Or, most likely, because it was a horse-drawn system that ran so gently that people would jump off to gather brambles or daisies before reboarding.

Walking down the tunnel, it doesn't feel quite so innocent – there is a noticeable drop in temperature and a strong draught whistling through. Back in the 1980s, when it first reopened, there were rumours that you could be knocked from your bike by garrotting wires strung across the path.

Were you able to enter the Scotland Street tunnel, you would find it airless, with an even steeper 1-in-27 slope, and at 910 metres, almost twice as long. The blocked-off entrance is in the north wall of Waverley Station. It runs below St Andrew Square, down Dublin Street, emerging in the King George V Park at the foot of Scotland Street (known locally as Scotland Yard).

Its creation was not so innocent: despite having employed top civil engineer George Buchanan to calm the public's fears about burrowing under their New Town houses, one of the tunnels went askew and a huge wave of water burst through the wall, flooding the houses in Canonmills and drowning four miners. Only two weeks after the tunnel opened in 1847, the rope hauling the trains snapped. Service was suspended. The guilty line was soon replaced by another route and closed only six years after opening.

SCIENNES JEWISH CEMETERY

Sciennes House Place, Edinburgh EH9 1NN
• Closed to the public but can be viewed through the railings
• Buses: 42, 67, 29

> *Scotland's first Jewish cemetery*

I n a hidden back street of Sciennes, tucked in between a row of tenements, a tiny graveyard was opened in 1816 by the Edinburgh Hebrew Congregation, whose synagogue is not far from here (see overleaf). It was for a long time the only Jewish cemetery in Scotland.

This street was then called Braid Place and there used to be a passage leading to the cemetery from Causewayside, charmingly called "Jew's Close", but it was demolished in the 1960s. Now the twenty or so ancient headstones are closed off to the public but can be viewed through the railings. Inscribed in Hebrew, and many worn away, the occasional name can be read in English – Lipman, Ezekiel, Ashenheim. Jewish families from all over Scotland purchased plots here, since at the time, there was no other consecrated ground north of the border.

The very first Jewish burial plot – a rocky cavern purchased by Herman Lyon for his family – was on the east side of the old City Observatory on Calton Hill. Lyon, who came from Germany in 1788, was a dentist and chiropodist – or "Corn Operator", as he described himself. Now all traces of the Calton Hill vault are gone, but some of his descendants lie here in Causewayside. Notable members of the Edinburgh Jewish community include the author Muriel Spark, the Nobel Prize-winning physicist Max born and Conservative politician Malcolm Rifkind.

In fact this area of Causewayside used to be the heart of a thriving Jewish community, with three kosher butchers, a kosher fish and chip shop in Davie Street, and Kleinberg the bakers in East Cross Causewayside. When they closed in 2005, if you wanted to buy kosher rye loaves or plaited challah bread, you had to get supermarket stuff shipped from Manchester. That is until Falko Konditormeister, the German bakery in Bruntsfield, stepped in to the unleavened gap. Now, every Friday morning, a member of the Jewish community goes to the branch to ignite the oven, and the master baker produces kosher-certified challah for Edinburgh's Shabbat dinners.

Sciennes Hill House, the building opposite the cemetery, was where Walter Scott met Robert Burns, who was weeping at the sight of Banbury's painting of a dead soldier. It was their one and only encounter.

לזכרון
האשה ריזא בת ר׳ אליעזר
נפטרה כ׳ ניסן תשי״ד

IN LOVING MEMORY OF
ROSA
WIFE OF DAVID OPPENHEIM
1878 – 1954

STAINED-GLASS WINDOWS OF EDINBURGH'S SYNAGOGUE

4a Salisbury Road, Edinburgh EH16 5AB
• www.ehcong.com
• Visits can be arranged in advance by emailing: secretary@ehcong.com (a small donation would be gratefully received)
• Buses: 2, 14, 30, 33

> **Windows on the soul**

It's easy to drive past Edinburgh's only synagogue, as you head west from the Royal Commonwealth Pool, and entirely miss this quietly special Art Deco *shul*. It has been standing there since 1932, when the Edinburgh Hebrew Congregation (EHC) was at its peak, filling the 2,000 seats inside.

The first recording of a Jewish resident in Edinburgh was in 1691. Gradually the population grew until, in 1825, the first synagogue was created not far from here in Richmond Court, seating sixty-seven people. By the turn of the century, there were four or five different synagogues peppered around the south side. Dr Salis Daiches, the then minister of the ECH, conceived of this *schul* to bring them all together.

Back when it was erected, it was the only red-brick building in Edinburgh. But its current Grade II listing is a result of its striking collection of stained-glass windows: the six in the small prayer hall are by Edinburgh-born William Wilson – one of Scotland's great artists – who worked in print, watercolour and stained glass. The other windows around the synagogue are by a variety of artists; two are by the architect Henry Joseph himself. But thirteen windows remain a mystery, despite extensive research by local historian Bobbi Smith. Depicting Hebrew biblical iconography such as the tribes of Israel, the Menorah and the Star of David, the windows were donated over the years by members of the congregation. Records were kept of the donors but, much to Smith's frustration, not of the artists who created them.

The Edinburgh Jewish community has now dwindled to under 150, so the EHC has had to halve the size of the main prayer hall. Some fear that within the next decade or so, the congregation may die out completely. But there are some rays of light glinting through. In 2009 several of the synagogue's windows were vandalised by two local Muslim youths. In response, an extraordinary act of solidarity came from the Scottish Islamic Foundation, which offered to guard the building and wrote to the ECH to say, "We wish you to know that the Muslim community stand full square with you in revulsion and horror at this vandalism. To violently damage any building is wrong. That this is a respected place of worship, faith and spirituality makes the crime even more heinous."

STATUE OF HUANG KUANG

Confucius Institute for Scotland, Abden House, 1 Marchhall Crescent,
Edinburgh EH16 5HP
• Tel: 0131 662 2180 • www.confuciusinstitute.ac.uk
• Statue viewable 24 hrs • Free
• Abden House viewable during office hours (Mon–Fri 9.30am–6pm),
though better to phone in advance
• Buses: 2, 14, 30, 33

*The first
Chinese student of
Western medicine*

H idden away next to Pollock Halls, in an area of Victorian housing called the Blacket, is a grand Jacobean house called Abden. It is the home of the Confucius Institute for Scotland – a quietly impressive body that promotes educational, economic and cultural ties between Scotland and China. The organisation has been behind all the most memorable Scottish Chinese cultural events, like the Terracotta Warrior Lanterns display in Old Quad, the Beijing Film Academy's production of *A Midsummer Night's Dream* and the UK-wide Cinema China film festival.

Opposite the front door is a 2-metre-high bronze statue of a modest-looking bespectacled man dressed in long Chinese robes, a book under his arm. It is the only statue of a student to be found anywhere in the university. His name is Huang Kuang, and he was the first Chinese student to study in the West. He received a PhD from Edinburgh's medical school in 1857, went on to introduce new forms of surgery to China and played a pivotal role in controlling the Canton cholera epidemic of 1870. The statue was presented to the Confucius Institute by the city of Zhuhai, in Guangdong province, and was unveiled in 2007 as part of the opening ceremony by former First Minister Alex Salmond.

Abden House itself is an interesting building that you can explore by appointment or if you attend any of the institute's many classes in Chinese language or calligraphy, or one of their business lectures. All the rooms have the amazing backdrop of Arthur's Seat towering through the windows. A small library has a collection of English/Chinese novels, and books on Chinese art, business, cooking, politics and religions, along with Chinese-language DVDs.

The drawing room has some beautiful Chinese-style wall paintings of birds and flowers by the Scottish artist Ursula Davidson. Interestingly, they were painted in 1967, pre-dating the arrival of the Confucius Institute by 40 years. At that time, the house was the official residence of the Principal and Vice-Chancellor of Edinburgh University.

THE BLACKET: EDINBURGH'S FIRST VILLA-BASED INNER SUBURB

Abden House is at the edge of what is called the Blacket conservation area: 5 streets consisting of 140 well-preserved grand Victorian villas. Basically, a very posh housing estate. Arthur Conan Doyle's teacher, Dr Joseph Bell, who was supposedly an early model for Sherlock Holmes, lived here. You can still see the five sets of "gate piers" – the pillars of the gatehouse lodges – surrounding the estate. The main piers are on the junction of Blacket Avenue with Minto Street at one end, and on Dalkeith Road at the other.

THE BORE STONE

In which the Royal Standard was last
pitched for the muster of the Scottish
army on the Borough-muir before the
Battle of Flodden
1513

BORE STANE

9

Opposite 122 Morningside Road, Edinburgh EH10 4BY
• Open 24 hrs. Admission free
• Buses: 5, 11, 15/15A, 16, 23, 36, 45

Marmion monument

Propped up just above head height in the wall of the former Morningside parish church on Morningside Road, just above the junction with Newbattle Terrace, is a very old lump of rock. A gilded plaque below tells you that this was the stone "In which the Royal Standard was last pitched for the muster of the Scottish army on the Burgh Muir before the Battle of Flodden, 1513".

It then quotes a passage from "Marmion", Sir Walter Scott's epic poem about an eponymous flawed hero who tries to get rid of his rival in love by falsely implicating him for treason. Marmion's plan backfires and he not only loses the girl but also meets his doom at Flodden – the most disastrous battle in Scottish history:

> *Highest and midmost was desiret,*
> *The Royal Banner floating wide,*
> *The staff a pine tree strong and straight,*
> *Pitch'd deeply in a massive stone,*
> *Which still in memory is shown,*
> *Yet bent beneath the Standards weight.*

A "bore stane" is a stone that has been bored to allow a flagstaff to be inserted. But this stone doesn't appear to have such a hole, let alone one large enough to take a pine tree. Historians suspect the Flodden tale was probably folklore made concrete in Scott's mythologisings and the stone was more likely the cover of a stone coffin or "cist". But it is located at what was the high point of the Burgh Muir, the 5 square miles (13 sq. km) of common land extending as far up as Forest Road, and as far east as Dalkeith Road. This was where the Scots kings used to train and gather their troops before battle, so a flag might well have been raised here.

Behind the stane is Morningside parish church, which has been converted into the drama department of Napier University. It is only officially open to the public when there is a performance (check: www.napier.ac.uk/acting), but see if they might let you in and you can get very close to some rather impressive tall stained-glass windows that are now hidden backstage on the north and south walls.

NEARBY

Morningside Road was the main road south, wide enough for horse-drawn coaches. If you cross the road and head down the hill, just on the junction with Morningside Place, you will find an ancient milestone embedded in the low curved wall which reads "One mile from Tollcross".

SPRINGVALLEY GARDENS

Morningside, Edinburgh EH10 4QG
• Viewable 24 hrs
• Admission free
• Buses: 11, 15, 15A, 23, 38, 41

> **Wild West cowboy street**

Most people in Morningside are unaware that just behind the main street is a little corner of the Wild West. Student filmmakers know about it – it has formed the backdrop for many a gun-slinging, whisky-sliding, whore-housing McWestern. John Hannah filmed a nightclub scene there for an episode of *Rebus*. Country & Western singers have shot their album covers and music videos in the alley. And even the occasional shotgun wedding has used it as a backdrop for photographs of the big day.

This rootin' tootin' street veneer was built in 1995 by Michael Faulkner, a furniture salesman who wanted a theme park for his "Pine Country" Southern-style wooden furniture. But this was no cowboy outfit. Michael's father was Lord Faulkner, briefly the last prime minister of Northern Ireland. Michael and wife Lynn McGregor – described as "right arty" by the proprietor of the neighbouring Lawnmower Services – hired some set-building friends, who'd just come back from working on EuroDisney, to build the perfect setting for their furniture emporium. Like a tiny frontier town, it took only a few months to go up, and fast became an artists' community, each one of the little timber-clad garages housing different craftspeople. It included a Jail, a Trading Station and a Cantina, which is actually the library's fire escape. Sadly, this grand and inventive vision was short-lived – only four years later, IKEA opened its swinging doors and the thriving carpentry business was sawdust.

Now it's only tumbleweed and mechanics passing by on their way to their garages. Bankrupt, Michael moved back to settle in his family's holiday house on the island of Islandmore. It was an even wilder West, without electricity or running water. But ever the entrepreneur, he built the place up and published a book, *The Blue Cabin*, documenting how he had survived this new frontier.

NEARBY

Embedded in the wall of the same yard are some curiously-shaped stones – crosses, arches and fleur-de-lys – that are of great interest to historians and architecture students. They are thought to be remnants of Holy Trinity, the 15th-century church of the college hospital which once stood on Leith Wynd, now the back of Waverley Station. If you take a wee gift for the lovely owners of Lawnmower Services (http://lawnmower-services-edinburgh.co.uk), they might even let you inside their repair shop to see the other holy fragments.

HIDDEN HERMITAGE

Old Hermitage House
- Hermitage of Braid, 69a Braid Road, Edinburgh EH10 6JF
- Tel: 0131 529 2401 • www.fohb.org
- Email: naturalheritageservice@edinburgh.gov.uk
- Admission free
- House open: Mon–Fri 9am–4pm, Sun and Public Holidays 12 noon–4pm
- Buses: 5, 11, 15, 16

Cooking up a murder

The Hermitage of Braid is a popular dog-walking spot in Morningside, but there are several secret treasures hidden to all but the most curious of hounds. Some may have bounded up the steep terraces of the 18th-century walled garden and found the impressive doocot (dovecote) at the top, big enough to house 1,965 pigeons' nests or a couple of medium-sized families. Others may have sniffed out the Victorian ice house, its small grated entrance hidden in the hillside above the big house, allowing game, sorbets and ice cream to be stored on ice, probably hacked from the duck pond.

More difficult to track down is the old water-pumping system in the Braid burn, between the stable block and the walled garden. Look carefully along the water's edge and you will spot two crumbling spherical brick structures that seem to have cannonballs at their centres. These were the valves from an ingenious hydraulic ram, which used the power of the stream to push water uphill into a storage tank. Water flowed from the burn into a wide pipe attached to a narrower pipe, which would build in pressure and suddenly shut off, creating a shock that forced water in the small pipe upwards. Once the pressure dropped again, the gate would reopen and the cycle was repeated. A highly practical if perhaps noisy system, which the friends of the Hermitage of Braid hope to restore and so supply the walled garden with water.

But the most intriguing fixture is located in the basement of Old Hermitage House, built by Charles Gordon of Cluny in 1775. Gordon was famously miserly and often "refused to get up out of bed on the ground that he could not afford it". Downstairs from the visitor centre, and along the end of the corridor, is a yellow-walled Victorian kitchen, oddly claustrophobic considering its large size. A Cookson cast iron range is built into the back wall, and next to it is the round, pitch-black door to a bread oven. Not so unusual. But look closer at the decoration on the front: what seems at first to be a dancing couple is actually a witch-like woman strangling a man. No one seems to know the origins of this image ... although one local man remembers hearing of a woman who murdered her husband and buried him in the flower bed in front of Old Hermitage House. Why Gordon would have gone to the expense of commemorating this tale on the kitchen appliances remains a mystery: perhaps he had a hand in the matter?

NEARBY

On the ground outside 66 Braid Road are the Hanging Stones, marking the spot where two highwaymen were hanged on 25 January 1815, the last execution in Scotland for highway robbery.

COCKBURN GEOLOGICAL MUSEUM

School of GeoSciences, The University of Edinburgh, Grant Institute,
King's Buildings, West Mains Road, Edinburgh EH9 3JW
• Tel: 0131 650 8536
• www.geos.ed.ac.uk/public/cockburn
• Email: cockburn.museum@ed.ac.uk
• Access free, by appointment only, and on Doors Open Day (Sept.)
• Buses: 24, 38, 41, 42, 67

Fossil fuel

What with Edinburgh's proud history of geology stretching back to the great man himself, James Hutton, it is not surprising that the School of Geosciences has an impressive collection of old rocks. This is a teaching museum so it's not advertised, but anyone can go if they make a request in advance. You will probably be shown round the displays by Gillian McCay, who has the most extraordinary things randomly stashed away in the desk drawers of her room: a fossilised ichthyosaur, the odd half-meteorite, and a flint axe head with its owner's name tag (Charles Lyell), one of the great godfathers of geology and the pivotal connection between Hutton and Darwin.

More carefully arranged in display cases are collections of minerals and fossils donated by Victorian gentlemen, like Dr James Currie, who loved the more blingy minerals: his shiny black lump of manganite resembles a crystalline clump of liquorice allsorts. Below each cabinet are drawer upon felt-lined drawer of labelled minerals. If there's a particular rock you're looking for, there'll be one here with its name on it.

In one corner is a white classical bust of an eminent gentleman. Nobody knows who the man is – it's a random sculpture rescued from a skip, because he looks a bit like the geologist Hugh Miller. But what the museum's curators are actually interested in is the black plinth below: a solid block of torbanite, a.k.a. boghead coal, the same oil shale which forms most of the bings around West Lothian (see p. 179).

Upstairs is a room lined with 3D plaster-cast topographical maps. One shows the area of Assynt, including Suilven, Quinaq and most importantly, the Moine Thrust, where layers of older rock have slipped over younger rock, creating, for a while, great geological confusion.

There's a fossil here of just about anything that ever moved. One of the most beautiful displays is of fossilised fish from Dura Den, their black scales and curved backbones swimming across slices of yellow sandstone. These were the fish that developed lobe-like fins and crawled out of the water. Well, things can get desperate in Fife.

And one last case contains an attractive set of geologists' tools – varying sizes of rock hammers, chisels and dusting brushes owned by Henry Cadell, who designed experimental equipment. In the corner is a small disc of rock with tiny circular indentations – the pitter patter of fossilised rain drops.

PHYLLIS BONE ZOOLOGICAL SCULPTURES ⓭

Ashworth Laboratories, King's Buildings, West Mains Road, Edinburgh
EH9 3JT
- www.nhc.ed.ac.uk
- Email: david.brown@ed.ac.uk
- Exterior viewable 24 hrs
- Free
- Buses: 24, 38, 41, 42, 67

A stone menagerie

All around the outside of the Ashworth Laboratories are small but beautifully carved animal sculptures. They were commissioned for the new zoology department, which in the 1920s was based at Old College and fast running out of space now that normal life was resuming post-war. James Ashworth, Professor of Natural History and specialist in the nerve fibres of polychaete worms, managed to persuade both the Carnegie Trust and J.D. Rockefeller to help fund the building of this state-of-the-art facility.

The resulting designs by Sir Robert Lorimer and John F. Matthews, based on Ashworth's sketches, were perfectly practical, spacious, evenly lit, but a little … dull. Enter Phyllis Bone, a graduate of Edinburgh College of Art who had been chosen by Lorimer to carve the animal sculptures for the Scottish National War Memorial. Bone had studied *animalier* under Édouard Navellier in Paris. Her work was both scientific in its detail and strikingly modern in style.

Bone modelled the animals in clay and worked with the Holyrood Pottery to have them cast in an artificial stone (a bit like Coade stone: see p. 242). Her creatures represent different zoogeographical regions: the reindeer, golden eagle and polar bear are from the Palaearctic region. A beaver and a bison come from the Nearctic. An aardvark, a chimpanzee and a lion signify the Ethiopian (now Afrotropical) region. The Oriental region, aka the Indomalaya ecozone, enlists a rhinoceros, a tiger and an elephant, with ropes entwining its great feet. From Australia we have a kangaroo, from South America a nine-banded armadillo, and from New Zealand a pair of sphenodon lizards. Invertebrates have a group of their own: a dung beetle, a crab and a swirling octopus.

On the main staircase inside the building are more of Bone's sculptures – tiny bronze owls, cats and monkeys perch on top of the finials of the metal balustrade. There is also a copy of Hugo Rheinhold's famous *Darwin's monkey* sculpture: a chimpanzee sitting atop a pile of books and contemplating a skull, probably wondering why he's been called a monkey, not an ape.

In 1944 Bone went on to become the first woman elected to the Royal Scottish Academy. Asked why it was always animals she sculpted, she replied: "All these creatures that fly from us shyly or threaten us fiercely interest me. I am enthralled by their shapes, their rhythmic movements, which, separately and combined, are so decorative and sculptural."

LIBERTON TOWER

7 Liberton Tower Lane (off Liberton Drive), Edinburgh EH16 6TQ
• www.libertontower.com
• Email: info@libertontower.com
• Entry free, by appointment
• Available to rent from £800.00 per week (winter) to £1,400.00 per week (Festivals, Christmas & New Year)
• Buses (10-min. walk): 7, 37, 47, 67

> *Head*
> *above*
> *the parapet*

A s holiday homes go, Liberton Tower is a pretty spectacular let. A golden-ochre fortress perched high on a hillside to the south of Edinburgh, its entrance door is 5 metres off the ground, reached by a long wooden external staircase leading halfway up the tower to the third floor. Originally it would have been a drop drawbridge over a moat, with a high star-shaped wall enclosure. They took their defences seriously back in the 1490s.

Now the place is a lot more welcoming, at least if it's not currently being rented out. You can have a look round on Doors Open Day in September or, if you're lucky, by appointment with Rod Berg, who not only manages the property but helped restore it. The main reception room is stone-flagged, with ochre-washed walls and wooden beamed ceilings. And yet it's cosy – the walls are a metre and a half thick and have only a few slit-like windows. Below the long dining table is an equally long trap door to the kitchen below, allowing the room to be served without constantly climbing the narrow staircase. Originally, there was a similar trapdoor from the kitchen down to the animal enclosure on the ground floor. Since there was no door down there, the animals were ungracefully hoisted up and down.

If you look carefully in the wall along from the entrance to the reception room, you will find a small hole. This is the "laird's lug", which would have been hidden behind a tapestry, allowing the owner to discreetly eavesdrop on his guests' conversations.

The laird's quarters were in the bedroom behind this wall, which also has the route up to the rooftop. Climb the ladder and you emerge onto the parapet walkway around the roof, with exhilarating views over the south of Edinburgh. You look down onto Blackford Tower to the west, and the contemporaneous Craigmillar Castle (see p. 231) to the east. Plus Edinburgh Castle, Fife, the Firth of Forth, East Lothian and out to the North Sea. So all approaching enemies could be spotted in good time.

In case you're imagining that the enemies in question were hoards of lepers, banging at the walls like a medieval zombie flick, the name "Liberton" (contrary to popular belief) does not derive from "Lepers' Town". It is probably so called because David I, King of Scotland in the 11th century, owned the land round there and the "freed men" he hired to farm it were called Libertines.

GILMERTON COVE

16 Drum Street, Gilmerton, Edinburgh EH17 8QH
• www.gilmertoncove.org.uk
• 1-hr tours by appointment only: Mon–Sun 10am–4pm
• Adult £7.50; concession £6.50; child (5–16) £4; family ticket £20.00
• Buses: 3, 7, 18, 29

"

> *A subterraneous uncertainty*

Underneath the main crossroads at Gilmerton, a small suburb to the south of Edinburgh, lies a network of underground caves known as Gilmerton Cove. It's easy to miss the entrance, which is opposite the Royal Bingo and one up from Ladbrokes bookies, housed in what was once a miner's cottage. Sign up for a tour and you will be equipped with a hard hat for low ceilings, and guided down the steps by torchlight into this ghostly grotto. Wear something warm; the walls seem to sweat a cold sheen and your breath condenses in the dim yellow light.

Despite extensive investigations, nobody really knows when, why or by whom this mysterious labyrinth of seven sandstone rooms was created. In 1724 a blacksmith called George Patterson claimed to have hewn his "underground house" out of the rock with his own hands in under five years, but apart from this being a near physical impossibility – this is not soft crumbling sandstone but the hard unyielding type – archaeologists say that it predates Mr Patterson by at least three hundred years, if not two thousand …

As there are stone pews, slab tables, a dungeon or well, carved symbols and deep bowl-shaped indentations cut into the rock table, several alternate theories as to its use have been proposed: (a) a place of worship for Roman soldiers stationed on the Braid Hills some two thousand years ago; (b) a secret chapel for the 1638 Covenanters who were outlawed by King Charles I; (c) a witches' coven, for which the Lothians were famous; (d) a secret den of various iniquities frequented by the Hellfire Club (the 18th-century equivalent of the Bullingdon Club); (e) a dissecting room for Burke and Hare's snatched bodies; (f) a Masonic hall or even a hangout for the Knights Templars; or (g) a torture chamber for a Fritzl-style quarryman. Gilmerton Heritage Trust would like to investigate further and break through some of the rubble-blocked passages, but unfortunately if they did so, Gilmerton crossroads would collapse. So until they save up enough cash to get the structural engineers in, they just have to keep ruminating over the ever-increasing list of roughly hewn theories …

BALM WELL OF ST CATHERINE

41 Howden Hall Road, Edinburgh EH16 6PG
• Open 24 hrs. Free
• Buses: 7, 37, 47, 67

Sticky dip

The most bizarre thing about the Balm Well of St Catherine is its location: at the back of the car park of the Toby Carvery pub in Liberton. Admittedly, it's a rather grand branch of Toby's, inhabiting what was once the home of Sir William Rae, the Lord Advocate who presided over the trial of serial killer William Burke.

Now it's a family-friendly pub, conveniently near the Moreton crematorium, and so many of its customers are not really in the mood for exploring the gardens. But if you do, you will find nestling in the grass what looks like a small stone mansion for fairy folk, its way barred and locked. The lintel over the top reads "1563" but there are records of it much earlier.

Inside you can see some leaves, stones, a few sticks, sitting in what appears to be stagnant black water. But it's not dirt on the surface: it's oil. Because the water that emerges here bubbles up through oil shale, extracting the bitumen from the layers of flaking sedimentary rock and floating it up to the surface.

Prior to this geological understanding, the explanation for the oil went as follows: in the 11th century, St Katherine (with a K) was bringing back some holy oil, which she'd carried all the way from Mount Sinai in Egypt, having collected it from the seeping corpse of the 4th-century martyr St Catherine (with a C) of Alexandria. As she crossed the Liberton Hill, Katherine-with-a-K stopped, presumably weary from her walk, and was so taken with the view of the city that she accidentally dropped the precious oil and it spilt into the soil. But there, miraculously, sprang a well with a never-ending supply of the black stuff.

Through the ages it was thought to be a cure for all cutaneous diseases, especially eczema, scabies and supposedly leprosy, but disappointingly it turns out that talk of Liberton being a leper colony is somewhat exaggerated. Less stricken visitors to the oily well include the 15th-century philosopher and poet Hector Boece; and also James IV, who had stone steps built in 1617, though Cromwell's soldiers destroyed all the stonework in 1650.

The current housing was erected in 1889 (the randomly dated lintel came from elsewhere). By this time shale oil had been discovered, the world's first mineral oil-processing plant had been established at Bathgate in 1851 and the holy power of the oily water gradually seeped away.

MALLENY GARDEN

Blue Cottage, Balerno, Edinburgh EH14 7AF
- Tel: 0131 449 2283
- www.nts.org.uk/Property/Malleny-Garden
- Open daily 10am–5pm (or sunset if earlier)
- Adult £3.50; family ticket £9.00; 1 parent £7.00; concessions £2.50; National Trust members free
- Buses: 44 [Lothian], 44, 66 [First Edinburgh]

> ***Secret garden of Balerno***

Tucked on the outskirts of Edinburgh behind Currie Rugby Club, Malleny Garden feels like the ultimate secret garden. You approach via a long woodland path crossing the Bavelaw Burn and enter through a small doorway with a dramatically designed spread eagle wrought-iron gate – the crest of the Gore Brown Hendersons, who bequeathed the garden to the Natural Trust for Scotland in 1968. As you descend the steps you pass another grand crest, that of the previous owners, the Roseberys, aka Primrose, hence the primrose motif. There is a lot of interesting decorative arts-and-crafts-style metalwork around, though much was taken off to Skirling House by Lord Carmichael.

The entrance to Malleny was once the croquet house; and the raised lawn before you (now broken up with little squares of brightly contrasting low red berberis hedges) was a croquet pitch. The wall around the garden creates a microclimate and gives protection from the chill Pentland winds – gardening in such a cold pocket requires great skill.

The centrepiece is provided by the ancient yew trees called the Four Apostles (or Evangelists), the last of what was once a group of twelve, planted around the garden in the 17th century, supposedly to commemorate the Union between Scotland and England. Now over 9 metres tall, a special cherry-picker crane which can squeeze in through the human-size gates is required to trim the tops.

A great long yew hedge splits the garden in two, north to south. You pass through it via a tall keyhole-shaped gap. And that's when the scent hits you – along the far wall of the lower half of the garden is the National Collection of 19th-century shrub roses. Among them are *Rosa spinosissima*, the Scotch Rose, and *Rosa sericea pteracantha* with its unusual red translucent thorns.

Before you leave, look for the beautiful green bird, perhaps a woodpecker or a kingfisher (on the wrought-iron gate), behind the fountain next door to the dovecote in front of the house.

> Malleny House itself is privately rented but occasionally the Georgian rooms are open to the public.

> Even more secret than the garden is the Scott Burial Vault, hidden in the woodlands north-east of the house. As you drive out on the one-way system, you come to a T-junction with the road you came in on. Directly opposite you is the pathway through the woods which leads you to the vault, though you can only view it from behind a locked gate.

SWANSTON VILLAGE

Above Swanston Brasserie, 111 Swanston Rd, Swanston, Edinburgh
EH10 7DS
• Visitable 24 hrs. Free admission. Parking free
• Nearest buses (15-min. walk): 4, 5, 15, 18, 27

Robert Louis Stevenson's municipal pleasure house

Swanston Village is an almost perfectly preserved 18th-century hamlet on the slopes of the Pentland Hills. Due to the lack of car access, it has managed to remain pretty much a secret for decades. Visitors must park by the brasserie/golf course below and take the short walk up through the woods to the cluster of whitewashed thatched cottages. Sit on the bench dedicated to the Orcadian-born poet Edwin Muir, who "liked to linger and meditate" here, and your view won't be much different from his. The ski slopes wouldn't have been here, but the Hare Burn was … and also the T-shaped woods, planted by the Trotter family.

But Swanston's most famous literary association is with Robert Louis Stevenson, who as a teenager loved to walk these hills. Hoping the fresh air would help with Robert's tuberculosis, his family rented a house just down from here. It's now privately owned so you can't enter, but you get a good view if you head back down past the brasserie and turn left, walking west along the bottom edge of the golf course, round the back of the livery stables and onto the footpath towards Dreghorn. On your right, across the gardens, you can see the large house which is misleadingly named Swanston Cottage. It was originally only a "but'n'ben" (two-roomed house) until it was developed by local councillors as a secret party venue, out of sight of Edinburgh's prying eyes. Stevenson wrote scathingly: "Long ago this sheltered field was purchased by the Edinburgh Magistrates for the sake of the springs that rise or gather there. After they had built their water house and layed their pipes, it occurred to them that the place was suitable for junketting. Once entertained, with jovial Magistrates and public funds, the idea led speedily to accomplishment: and Edinburgh could soon boast of a municipal pleasure house."

The lily ponds in the gardens below were the filter tanks for Edinburgh's first piped water supply. You can go down and see the 1761 water house RLS mentions at the foot of the driveway by the Waterman's Cottage. The waterman was the brother of Stevenson's nanny, Alison Cunningham, known as "Cummy". For a while she lived here too: her dates "AC 1880–1893" are engraved over the door. Sadly, the fresh air failed to cure RLS and he eventually moved to Samoa in search of better health. He died there aged only 44, nicknamed "Tusitala" by the locals: teller of tales.

SECRET HERB GARDEN

32A Old Pentland Road, Edinburgh EH10 7EA
- Tel: 07525 069 773 or 07768 530 044
- www.secretherbgarden.co.uk
- Email: admin@secretherbgarden.co.uk
- Open daily: 10am–4pm. Admission free
- Buses: 15, 47, 67 (+ 15-min. walk)

Organic spread

T hough it's only a *Kulört* decorative stone's throw away from the Loanhead IKEA warehouse, visiting the Secret Herb Garden is like dropping into a parallel universe. There's no incomprehensible one-way system or checkout array with 25-metre queues. The whole place is very laid-back, with saggy old armchairs dozing in the greenhouse under flopping arms of ripening tomatoes. You can wander around the 3-hectare site freely, scratch and sniff the vast array of organically farmed herbs, and follow your nose to find the occasional herbal secret.

Sniff out the very Herbie VW, sprouting with chamomile, lavender and thyme. Or the brown and yellow stripy bee observatory, where you can watch the bees charging up and down their thickly planted wild flower pollen run. Or the "Tub" – an oil tank turned on its side, scrubbed out and converted into a beautiful little cabin, hireable for small group activities like yoga classes or therapy sessions.

In the classroom, the owners run all sorts of herb, craft and therapy courses, from bee-keeping to raw chocolate-making. On summer evenings, they hold Full Moon Dinners, where top restaurateurs like the Balmoral and the Timberyard host outdoor feasts. And recently they've added New Moon events: more informal affairs with live music, street food and a craft beer bar.

Since their very first date, wine merchant Hamish and banking resource manager Liberty had fantasised about leaving their jobs and setting up a herbal paradise. Hamish spotted the site in passing – a derelict glasshouse completely overgrown with Rosebay Willowherb. He left a note with neighbours and soon he and Liberty were turning their pipe dream into a reality. For the first five years they lived in a static caravan, with four kids and five dogs. They've finally moved into a house they built on site – but they haven't stopped conjuring up dreams. They are converting an old taxi into a picnic spot, and also plan to turn the potting shed into a bar, plant a vineyard and bottle their own vintage. Soon IKEA will look like a corner shop by comparison.

NEARBY

Five minutes east of here is the hidden entrance to the Old Pentland Kirkyard, an ancient graveyard where many Covenanters were buried after their massacre at the battle of Rullion Green. Inside the watch house are the Arnold Stones, thought to date back to the 13th/14th centuries and to be symbols of the crusading Knights Templar, who had their headquarters only 20 minutes south of here at the town called Temple.

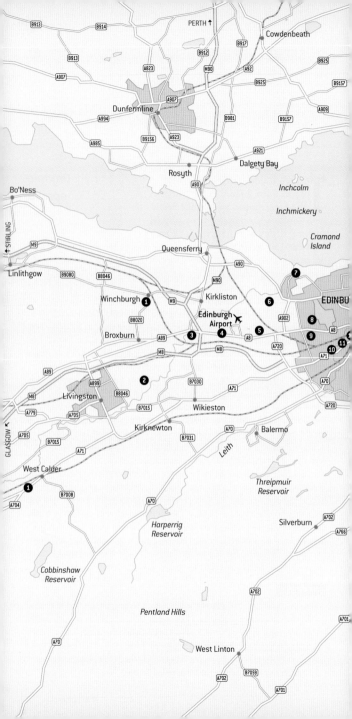

WEST

OIL-SHALE BINGS

Sites around West Lothian
• Accessible 24 hrs • Free
Five Sisters bing and Addiewell Nature Reserve, north-east of Addiewell,
Edinburgh EH55
Greendykes bing, Faucheldean bing and Niddry Castle bing near
Winchburgh, Edinburgh EH52

**Bings
sing**

The huge oil-shale bings are a familiar sight to anyone driving west out of Edinburgh. Along the side of the M8 and M9, giant reddish Toblerone slabs seem to have landed on the otherwise flattish countryside, like a child's drawing or an 8-bit graphic of a mountain range. Many people saw them as a terrible eyesore, shameful evidence of our rape of nature in the crude rush for oil. In 1851 Glasgow-born James "Paraffin" Young had developed his technique to distil oil from kerogen-rich sedimentary rock by heating it to 500 °C, lighting Britain's homes and half the streets of London with his paraffin oil and candle wax.

Scotland became the centre of shale-oil production, and for 100 years West Lothian's seams of lamosite and torbanite were torn from the ground, producing a million barrels of crude oil annually. But for every 10 barrels of oil, 7 tonnes of sterile, bluey-grey "blaes" waste was produced. This got dumped in heaps up to a height of 95 metres, gradually turning dusky pink as it oxidised. Whole buildings were engulfed – the elegant Westwood House is buried beneath peaks of the Five Sisters bing.

The discovery of more cheaply extracted petroleum brought the oil-shale industry to a standstill in the 1960s. But the vast and silent bings continued their quiet transformation. Some of the shale was used as hardcore for road building, but that hardly put a dent in them. Slowly, wind, rain and frost eroded the surfaces, and lichens and mosses started to colonise the alien landscape. Due to the unusual alkalinity and good drainage, rare strains of plants started to thrive. Soon botanists were studying the unusual flora and fauna. The bings at Addiewell and Faucheldean, where rare orchids and stag's-horn clubmoss grow, were declared a nature reserve, while Greendykes and the Five Sisters were scheduled national monuments.

If you fancy a spot of bing bagging, you can get into the biggest one, Greendykes, via paths from the Pavo Steel works and the eastern end of the Corecut works. Wear good supportive boots and take care as you're clambering around – the surfaces are still very loose scree and it's easy to twist an ankle. But they are amazing places to explore – you could be walking on Mars or trekking through the set of a Tattie Western: you can almost hear strains of an Ennio Morricone theme whistling round the slopes. But when you get to the top, try hard to resist the urge to shout Bingo.

If you want to learn more, go to the Museum of the Scottish Shale Oil Industry, in the Almond Valley Heritage Trust, Millfield, Livingston, West Lothian. EH54 7AR

KIRKHILL PILLAR

Almondell Country Park, Edinburgh EH52 5PE
- Tel: 01506 882 254
- www.westlothian.gov.uk/article/2060/Almondell-Calderwood-Country-Park
- almondell&calderwood@westlothian.gov.uk
- Park open dawn to dusk • Admission free
- Visitor Centre opening times: summer 9am–5pm, winter 10am–4pm
- No close bus route, nearest: 27 (to Raw Cottages near East Calder)
- Nearest train station: Uphall

*Cosmic
calculator
column*

I n front of the Almondell Country Park Visitor Centre is a pillar. It doesn't look very remarkable at first, just a tall stone post topped with a small belfry and an iron cross. But if you inspect it more closely, you will see that it is covered with Latin phrases, measurements and symbols, chiselled into the stone like the scrawlings of a fevered mathematician stonemason.

The pillar originally stood in the grounds of Kirkhill House, 5 km north of here. It was commissioned in 1776 by David Stewart Erskine, the 11th Earl of Buchan, to commemorate his own achievement: that of building a scale model of the solar system in his garden. In the tradition of the Enlightenment, Buchan was a lover of all the arts and sciences, but he also seems to have had an eye on his place in history. Sir Walter Scott described him as a person "whose immense vanity, bordering upon insanity, obscured, or rather eclipsed, very considerable talents …"

Whether it was inspired by ego or enthusiasm, sadly the laws of entropy have caused Buchan's giant orary to vanish into the cosmos, and the pillar's writing has become so worn that it's difficult to read. On the east side, the abbreviated text states: "In the year 1776, I caused a representation to be made of the solar system on a scale of 12.283 miles and 23/100 to an inch; the table of which epitome is engraved on a belfry which stands in the middle of the garden, and of which I shall insert a transcription below."

Said table lists the astronomical symbols for the sun and the planets (apart from Neptune, Uranus and Pluto, which had yet to be discovered) along with their scaled size and distance from the sun. Why Buchan chose such a peculiar scale is not known. But apparently much of the astronomical detail is remarkably accurate. It includes a prediction of the position of the planets on 20 February 2255. (According to Star Trek, that is when the Treaty of Armens is established between the Sheliak Corporate and the United Federation of Planets.)

Buchan would perhaps be pleased to know that he had inspired the Kirkhill Pillar Project, where local artists have created an artwalk through pieces inspired by the different planets. One of them, *Uranus*, is on the main road down into Almondell Park. Directions to the others can be found on their website: www.kirkhillpillarproject.org.uk

HULLY HILL CAIRN

Old Liston Road, Newbridge, Edinburgh EH28 8PH
• Open 24 hrs
• Admission free
• Bus: 63

*Stones
unturned*

Twixt the lines of the M8, M9, A8 and A89, where the Easyjets rise and the twin signs of BP and McDonald's sway, lies one of the most important prehistoric sites in southern Scotland. To find it, head to Newbridge roundabout and take the exit marked "Newbridge Industrial Estates", following the sign for such attractions as the Indoor Karting Centre and the Climbing Arena. Hully Hill Cairn is not signposted, but she's there on your right, in the field across from the petrol station.

She's an early Bronze Age burial mound surrounded by three Neolithic standing stones, gracefully ignoring the temporary irritations of fast food, slow traffic and "Xtreme Karting". A modern stone retaining wall has been wrapped around the mound, perhaps to stop it collapsing from sheer despair at what the last century has had to offer. This entire industrial zone was once a magnificent burial site, and just south of here an Iron Age chariot was excavated. It had been ceremonially buried intact. The standing stones predate the mound by about a thousand years and are the remains of what would have been a large stone circle. Archaeologists refer to them alphabetically but think of them, perhaps, as Annie, Barbara and Carol. There's also a fourth stone, the tall lozenge-shaped Doris, who has been left stranded on the other side of the roundabout, in the grounds of Exova testing. You can cross the motorway footbridge and wave to her across the dual carriageway or you can visit Exova (EH28 8PL), who will let you through to give Doris a comforting pat.

There's another ancient standing stone which was probably part of the same complex, right by the main runway of Edinburgh airport. This one's got an official name – the Cat Staine. You might be able to see it from your plane, but since the direction of take-off changes depending on the prevailing wind, it's 50/50 as to whether your seat is on the correct side for viewing. If you're taking off with the building on your right-hand side, the stone will be on your left at the start of your run.

Otherwise you can try and see it through the airport perimeter fence from the bank of the River Almond. You could drive to the bridge by Carlowrie Castle (EH29 9ES) and then walk east along the nearside of the river. Look for the stone just after a tributary on the right, beyond the perimeter fence. She'll be here long after all this mess has gone.

AIRPORT PRAYER AND QUIET ROOM ④

Ground floor, Edinburgh Airport, Edinburgh EH12 9DN
• www.edinburghairport.com
• Buses: 35, 100, C100, N22
• Tram stop: Edinburgh Airport
• Open during airport hours. Free entry

Flying visit

With everyone rushing to or from flights in a state of anxiety or exhaustion, very few people notice that there is a small room for quiet contemplation or prayer: it's hidden on the ground floor of the airport, next to the international arrivals area.

Often when you go in, the place is completely empty. It is laid out like a simple chapel, with a few rows of chairs facing a plain lectern, behind which is a circular blue stained-glass window, lit artificially. At the back is a stained-

glass wall, a patchwork of matching glass squares. In a shelf to the side are prayer mats and religious textbooks. Below your feet is a thick carpet to muffle the clack of heels that might interrupt meditation.

You can project whatever you wish into the space. It doesn't have to be religious contemplation. You can just take time to de-stress after security scrutiny, baggage excesses and legroom wars. Or indeed build up to them. I thought a friend with an acute phobia of flying might have appreciated the pre-flight calm but he felt the associations with funerals and eternity would be too melodramatic.

Stuart Greig, who made the "Inside Edinburgh Airport" documentary series, says the quiet room is often used by people with medical conditions who need a quiet place to sit before going through security, like a young man they filmed who had an extreme sensitivity to crowds and noise. But apparently the airport staff are aware that the quiet room has sometimes been used for distinctly unreligious activity. Knees, apparently, are not just for praying …

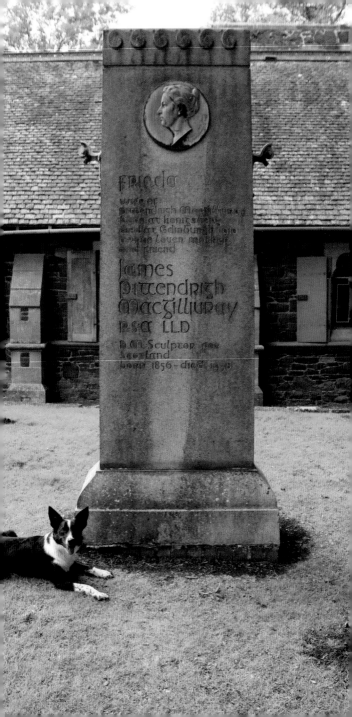

GOGAR CABINETWORKS

194 Glasgow Road, Edinburgh EH12 9BR
- Tel: 0131 317 7240
- Email: christopherscotland@yahoo.co.uk
- Graveyard and exterior open daylight hours
- Visitors to the workshop are always welcome by appointment
- Admission free
- Buses: 20, 35, 63. Tram stop: Gogarburn

> *The People's Democratic Republic of Gogarburn*

Gogar Old Kirk is now the last building left standing in its vicinity by the Gogarburn tram stop. All the other buildings which used to surround it – three cottages and an old listed smiddy – were torn down so that the Royal Bank of Scotland could have its own tram service. However, it has actually turned out to be the personal tram stop of the Old Kirk and its residents, the Gogar Cabinetworks – three designer-carpenters of bespoke hardwood furniture. They deserve the personal transportation reward as they spent six years surrounded by a giant building site, with the prospect of completion constantly receding. Sadly, Chris Holmes, who rescued the church from ruin in 1979 by repurposing it as a carpentry shop, died before the tramworks (a term which he said should be used in the loosest possible sense) were completed. But now Chris Scotland, who has been there since 1989, rather likes the tram he once railed against. Uses it quite often. Only problem is that whenever a tram passes the kirk, the internet cuts out. That's every fifteen minutes.

If you jump off at Gogarburn you can wander in any time to explore the grounds. There has been a church on this site since the 1200s, when it was part of the village of Nether Gogar. The current church and tower were a rather skilful 1890 bolt-on, and if you look at the walls carefully you can see the seam between the old and the new, where the rough boulder stonework suddenly becomes immaculately-joined sand and whinstone.

The graveyard contains some rather distinguished residents. There is the monument to the notable Victorian railway engineer Thomas Grainger. And the Scottish sculptor James Pittendrigh MacGillivray, who carved figures like John Knox and Robert Burns as well as his own very elegant tombstone. Elsewhere lies Colin Campbell Mitchell, who invented the Steam Catapult engine, which launched planes from aircraft carriers; and Sir Robert Liston, diplomat, ambassador and friend of George Washington.

If you are serious about buying something, you can knock on the door of the kirk and have a chat with one of the carpenters; they're a nice bunch. Or you can wander across the RBS bridge (renamed "The People's Democratic Republic of Gogarburn Flyover") and see how long it takes the security guards to rugby tackle you. Shouldn't have built that tram stop so close by, should they?

Gogar may be an old Celtic word for a small spur of land, or it may derive from "gowk", an old Lowland Scots word for cuckoo, commonly used to mean fool.

CAMMO ESTATE

Cammo Road, Edinburgh EH4 8AW
• Accessible 24 hrs (free) via the car park on Cammo Walk on the southern edge, by the north gate on the north-east side and by the main gate on the east side
• Buses: 31, 41

> *Edinburgh's Grey Gardens*

Tucked away between Barnton and Edinburgh airport lies the Cammo Estate, a beautiful place for a walk and hardly known outside the local area. It has a dramatic air of faded glory, with the wild grasses enveloping the ruins of Cammo House, the walled garden, ornamental canal, ha-ha and stables. The best-preserved feature is the castellated water tower which stands, now minus its sails, like an escaped chess piece on the side of the estate.

The original house was built in 1693 for John Menzies and is thought to be the inspiration for the House of Shaws in Robert Louis Stevenson's *Kidnapped* (though the houses of Pilrig and Cramond also vie for that title). The grounds are the work of Sir John Clerk, who bought the house in 1710 and created Scotland's first landscaped garden, seeking harmony with nature, rather than attempting to regulate it. He planted the beautiful deciduous woodlands, which include some of the oldest trees in Scotland.

But the story of how the once palatial house became a ruin is Edinburgh's own version of *Grey Gardens*. At the turn of the twentieth century, Cammo was purchased by the wealthy Mrs Clark, who lived there with her younger son Percival. He had a badly deformed spine and preferred the company of dogs to less tolerant humans. Mrs Clark had divorced her adulterous husband and changed her name to Maitland-Tennant. But she was known locally as the "black widow", only ever glimpsed through the drawn curtains of her black car as Percy chauffeured her to the bank.

She disinherited her oldest son Robert for leaving them, and deliberately ran the estate down, convinced he would try to overturn her will. When she died in 1955, Percy couldn't look after himself and moved into the farm lodge where he could be cared for, leaving the grand house with all its valuables for his beloved pack of forty-odd stray dogs to live in. Each day, he would let the dogs out in batches, room by room, and visit his mother's grave in the Pinetum just west of the house, marked by a large carpet of daffodils.

Left to the dogs, the house started to implode under the corrosive weight of excrement. Burglars "liberated" any valuables they could find. Arsonists did the rest. When Percy died in 1975, he left the rotting house and grounds to the National Trust as a public park – and now a dog-walkers' paradise.

LITTLE GATEHOUSE GALLERY

Gatehouse of Cramond Kirk, Cramond Glebe Road, Edinburgh EH4 6NS
• Tel: 07591 636759
• www.thelittlegatehousegallery.com
• Open: summer: 12 noon–5pm, daily except Wed. Winter: 12 noon–5pm Thurs–Sunday plus Monday Bank Holidays. Admission free
• Bus: 41

Basil Spence's student project

This has got to be Edinburgh's smallest art gallery. Okay, there will be some short-lived contender popping up in a police box somewhere during the Edinburgh Fringe. But this stone gatehouse of Cramond Kirk, measuring only 4 x 2.5 metres, was restored by the architect Sir Basil Spence in 1932, while he was still a student at Edinburgh College of Art and long before he designed the famous Coventry Cathedral. On the gable wall facing the street is a carved stone bell, which commemorates the fact that there was once a school here.

Originally a watch house to guard the graves from being robbed, the gatehouse became the Kirk's counting house.

Then, in 2014, local painter Ronald Ryan set it up as a miniature gallery specialising in paintings and prints, many by local artists. Two of those artists, Ferris Wood and the late Sax Shaw, were friends of Basil Spence. Sax Shaw was a Scottish post-war artist particularly famed for his stained glass and his tapestry work. He was director of the Dovecot tapestry studios, head of stained glass at Edinburgh College of Art and consultant to Basil Spence on the Coventry Cathedral tapestry.

Several of Shaw's watercolours are on display in the Little Gatehouse, which also has a portrait of him by Ryan painted in 1995.

The gallery also has a series of paintings of the ruins of the old iron mill, further up the River Almond, which Ryan has painted in spring, summer, autumn and winter. The iron mill was owned by the Cadell family from 1771 to 1860, and if you wander through the graveyard behind the gallery, you will find some rather unusual cast-iron grave markers. The largest of them, an iron obelisk painted white, is the Cadell family monument.

One of the names listed on the side is that of Anne Wilson, wife of Alex Cadell. Returning home slightly worse for wear after an 1851 New Year party, she was determined to take a short cut over the rocky outcrop between Cramond and Cramond Brig (now the location of the Salveson Steps), where she tragically slipped and drowned in the icy waters.

As well as making spades, shovels and nails, the Cadells made less innocent ironware, principally the shackles for slave boats, a fact which they seem not to have advertised. At one point, they thought that cast-iron grave markers would prove a major money-spinner, but they never caught on and they remain a rarity in graveyards.

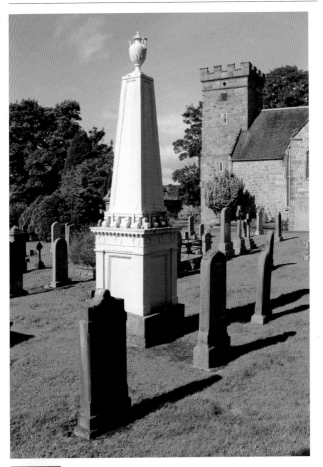

NEARBY

TWO RONNIES

Walk on through the archway in the wall on the opposite side of the kirk yard, and you emerge into the grounds of the Kirk Hall. Inside, you will find

a granite fish – a sculpture by the other Ronnie, artist Ronald Rae, who spent twenty years carving his sculptures in the grounds of Cramond Kirk. His giant fish sculpture twists on the Cramond shore here; his baby elephant has stomped around Edinburgh Airport; and his lion prowls in St Andrew Square Garden.

CORSTORPHINE HILL WALLED GARDEN

Clermiston Road, opposite Clerwood Terrace, Edinburgh EH12 8PG
- Open 8/9am to dusk most days
- www.corstorphinehill.org.uk
- Buses: 1, 21, 26

Hillside suntrap

Corstorphine Hill has lots of great finds strewn about its paths. There's the Clermiston Tower at the top, a monument to Sir Walter Scott, which intriguingly lines up with Cairn Papple and Cammo Tower (see p. 189) to the west.

North of the tower are some mysterious cup marks on the sloping rock surface – nine in the shape of a pentagon and two in the centre – which may be sacred markings dating back to the Neolithic or Bronze Age.

And on the west side of the hill is the secret garden – the old walled garden which once belonged to Hillwood House, the adjacent mansion that recently sold for £4 million and used to be owned by the makers of the Drambuie whisky liqueur. Word has it that some of the secret herbs and spices that produce its distinctive flavour were grown in this garden.

The garden is opened and closed each day by volunteers, so forgive them if sometimes the hours aren't exact. The best time to visit is on a sunny afternoon, when the west-facing slope captures all the sun's warmth. The three levels of sloping beds are filled with heathers, roses and wild flowers, dotted with crab apple, cherry and beech trees. Insects are encouraged with little "insect hotels" hiding in the corners. At the bottom is a pond with a wooden bridge, and a great wall wrapped around it and sheltering it from the elements. Though it was derelict for a long time, the whole area was lovingly restored by the Friends of Corstorphine Hill back in 2003.

If you look carefully, you'll see that the top wall is a geological jigsaw puzzle, containing carefully placed examples of all the local igneous and sedimentary stoneware: fragments of dolerite and gabbro; rippled red and white sandstone; grey, rusty-weathering mudstone … many containing patterns caused by fossilised plant remains.

> The paths that criss-cross the hill are a favourite for walkers and bikers, though in 2013 one of them had a rather gruesome encounter with the decomposed face of a woman staring up at him from the earth. Her dismembered body had been buried here by her son, whom she was visiting at his home on Balgreen Road.

THE DOWER HOUSE

⑨

1a Orchardfield Avenue, Edinburgh EH12 7SX
• Open Wed and Sat mornings 10am–12 noon. Admission free
• Buses: 1, 12, 26, 31

Home of the Ogre from Gogar

The house that stands in the corner of St Margaret's Park, Corstorphine, is one of the oldest inhabited buildings in Edinburgh, dating back to 1587. However, it seems the place is wrongly named, as a dower house is traditionally built to allow the Laird to kick out his father's widow, or dowager, and have the run of the castle himself. But there are no records of the Lords Forrester of Corstorphine Castle using the building in this way.

This tall lime-harled building, with its thick walls and small irregular windows, is now the Corstorphine Heritage Centre, which has created a little museum in the rooms spiralling off the steep narrow stone stairwell.

Here you will find all kinds of intriguing objects from Corstorphine's history. In the café on the ground floor is a wonderfully gruesome carved stone head with satanic horns, known locally as the "Ogre from Gogar", which was found in 1842 by two boys on the building site of the Gogar railway station.

On the wall upstairs you can see Harry Wright's *Fishing Birds* tapestry from

the Dovecot Tapestry Studio, which was originally located just around the corner in the house behind the Dovecot before it moved to its new Infirmary Street residence.

Up another floor and you'll find one of the most intriguing exhibits: a slice from the Corstorphine Sycamore, which was reputedly more than 400 years old when it was brought down in a storm in 1988. Pinpointed on its rings are historically important dates through which the tree lived, such as Edinburgh boy Alexander Graham Bell's 1876 invention of the telephone, and the 1859 publishing of *On the Origin of Species* – Charles Darwin being an ex-Edinburgh student. And before all that, when the great tree was but a sapling, the murder of the 2nd Lord Forrester in 1679 by his niece and lover, Lady Christine Nimmo (see below).

THE WHITE LADY OF CORSTORPHINE

The 2nd Lord Forrester was James Baillie, a rather laid-back laird of the castle, who was a drinker and womaniser and conducted many affairs behind his wife's back. One of his lovers was his own niece, Lady Christine Nimmo, who was also married. They would arrange to meet in secret by the sycamore tree, but one fateful night he failed to turn up. Lady Christine had a servant fetch him from the Black Bull Inn, but he arrived blind drunk and furious at having been summoned away from his pals. In the ensuing row, he somehow got stabbed in the stomach and bled to death on the ground. Lady Christine claimed that he ran at her with his sword, she grabbed it in self-defence and he accidentally fell on it. But she was sentenced to death and, despite escaping custody twice, she was beheaded at the Mercat Cross. But this was not punishment enough for such unwomanly behaviour, so she was doomed to forever wander the castle hallways in her white dress, holding her lover's blood-drenched sword. The castle was destroyed in the late 18th century, but the White Lady has been spotted since, obediently carrying out her post-death sentence by the dovecot near where the Corstorphine Sycamore once stood.

SAUGHTON PARK AND WINTER GARDENS

Entrances on Balgreen Road, Gorgie Road, Stevenson Drive and Fords
Road, Edinburgh EH11 3BQ
- Tel: 0131 529 7921
- www.edinburgh.gov.uk/saughtonpark
- Check website for opening times as they vary
- Buses: 1, 2, 3, 22, 25, 30, 35, 38

Empirical evidence

Saughton Park is a wonderful but sadly overlooked municipal park, as it is full of surprising jewels. You can enter via the country's oldest surviving ferro-concrete bridge, wander through a garden of sweet fragrances for the blind, and encounter Mahatma Gandhi nestling among the tropical greenery of the Winter Gardens.

At first sight, the area's connection with the pacifist leader of Indian independence might seem somewhat tenuous. His statue was commissioned in 1997 by local councillor Eric Milligan as it was fifty years since India and Pakistan had become independent and yet remained part of the Commonwealth, and all the Commonwealth heads of state were in town for their biennial summit. Milligan figured that Gandhi, very much a man of the people, wouldn't mind being placed a little further away from Edinburgh's centres of power and affluence. The statue was unveiled by none less than the Indian prime minister, Inder Kumar Gujral, who despite being a teetotaller, raised a glass of the local India Pale Ale to mark the occasion.

Wander on and you will find, bursting through the foliage, the ample bosom of the universal mother and personification of divine feminine creative power, the Hindu goddess Shakti – a gift from Professor and Mrs N. Rangabashyam, inspired by Milligan's event.

The gardens were once the grounds of the Saughton Estate, a grand 17th-century mansion. In 1824 the house was rented by the Institute for the Recovery of the Insane, where Dr William Lowe and Sir John Batty Tuke advocated better treatment of those with mental illnesses. Dr Lowe pioneered gardening as therapy, and so his patients are partly responsible for the gardens being so beautiful. The term "occupational therapy" was coined here.

The gardens were transformed for the Scottish National Exhibition in 1908, which is when the Winter Gardens glasshouses were built. Among the sights were a 60-foot (18-metre) drop of the water chute, a Moulin Rouge-themed helter-skelter and, more questionably, a Senegalese tribe, who had been uprooted and given a replica mud-hut village to live in. A baby born during their six-month stay was christened "Scotia Reekie" for the amusement of the public. You can see amazing archive footage of the crowds and the tribe on the National Libraries Scotland website: ssa.nls.uk/film/1699.

MERCHISTON TOWER CEILING

10 Colinton Road, Edinburgh EH10 5DT
• Visits by appointment only. Contact: press@napier.ac.uk
• Buses: 11, 15, 16, 23, 36, 45

*Rabelaisian
rafters*

There is something rather extraordinary hidden in the Merchiston Tower. The building itself is worthy of an entry: a medieval red stone tower house hidden in the middle of a modern university campus. It was the seat of Clan Napier and the birthplace of John Napier, the eighth Laird of Merchiston, mathematician, philosopher, inventor of logarithms, and after whom the university was named.

Climb the winding stone steps and you will find a large boardroom with an impressive long asymmetric table sitting on a split-pea green carpet; below is a minstrels' gallery. You are getting warmer. But it's not until you lean your head back that you really hit the hot stuff.

Look closely at the ceiling above you. Running along the rough pine boards are some rather unusual hand-painted tempera illustrations. They appear, at first sight, to be ornamental vases, flowers, angels. The explanatory notes on the wall tell you that this is the finest and earliest dated Scottish Renaissance ceiling from 1581, which was transferred here after being discovered at Prestongrange in 1962.

But then you start to notice the details: a winged lizard with a human head, a weird-looking angel emerging from a contorted shell, a bare-breasted Viking lass with a lion's-head door knocker hanging from her nether regions. It's all starting to get a bit Hieronymus Bosch.

And that's when you spot the pornographic elves. Truth be told, you shouldn't have climbed up to the minstrels' gallery and stood on a chair to see them. You got too close. And now it's too late. You'll never be able to think of Santa's little helpers in the same way again.

The bawdy images are copies of a 1565 French collection of woodcuts called "The Droll Dreams of Pantagruel", the work of François Desprez. He himself was inspired by a series of five books collectively entitled *The*

Life of Gargantua and Pantagruel by the satirist François Rabelais, which charts the epic and somewhat scatological adventures of two giants, father and son. The text is full of lively escapades. An entire civilisation is discovered living behind Pantagruel's teeth. He drowns an army in urine. He meets the Chitterlings: a race of half-men, half-sausages. Salvador Dalí published his depictions of the same characters in 1974. How they ended up on an East Lothian nobleman's ceiling is certainly worthy of more study.

SPRINGWELL HOUSE

1 Gorgie Road, Edinburgh EH11 2LA
• Viewable from the street, 24 hrs
• Buses: 1, 2, 3, 4, 25, 33, 44

> *Magdalene morality*

Springwell House, the imposing Victorian-school-style building set back from the corner of Gorgie Road, is currently being converted into luxury flats. Below the sharp crow steps of the roof windows, a placard proudly announces that its foundation stone was laid by the Lord Provost in 1863. But the history of Springwell House is not necessarily something to crow about. Because this was the Edinburgh Magdalene Asylum, where "fallen women anxious to reform" – i.e. sex workers and the "sexually promiscuous", so-labelled simply for having sex before marriage – were cleansed, re-educated and repackaged, often as maids for big houses.

The asylum was originally housed in a now demolished building on the Canongate, next to the Tolbooth Wynd. Women who had come in hope of finding a refuge from prostitution were kept in solitary confinement for the first three months "to eradicate the taint of moral contagion". They were then subject to bullying, torture and abuse by the staff, and stigmatisation by the public, who easily recognised them due to their shaven heads and plain smocks. In 1828, the day after being released from a year and a half in the asylum, Mary Patterson was murdered by Burke and Hare (see p. 141). She was 18.

In 1840 a new director was appointed: Dr William Tait. Despite his

slightly more enlightened attitude, he regarded prostitution as "wickedness", an evil to which gentlemen of good repute often unwittingly exposed themselves. It was Tait who decided that the asylum should move away from the city into the rural district of Dalry, arguing that the atmosphere of violence caused depression and a loss of self-respect among the women. But the idea that it was the women who were to blame and needed re-educating prevailed. The institution remained in Dalry until it went bankrupt and got taken over by Edinburgh Council, who turned it into a social work centre.

NEARBY

Down the side of Dalry Cemetery is a long, narrow, high walled passage with the atmospheric name Coffin Lane. The gravediggers used to drink at the nearby Athletic Arms, so the pub is known locally as "Diggers". It refused to serve women, or anything other than cask-strength 80-shilling beer.

OLD EDINBURGH MEAT MARKET

80 Fountainbridge, Edinburgh EH3 9QA
• Viewable 24 hrs
• Admission free
• Buses: 1, 34, 35, 47

Slaughterhouse 3

As you walk west along Fountainbridge, past the cream stone and brown glass office developments of Exchange Place, you will find an impressive double sandstone archway spanning the gap just before Chalmers Buildings. Beautifully carved bulls' heads protrude from the top of each arch and the words chiselled above read "1884 Edinburgh Meat Market".

Wander down the bollarded access street behind and you will find yourself in a little square between the office buildings with a large and rather unusual mural – a black and white photograph etched into 8-metre-long concrete panelling. It shows cattle being driven down the street here over a century ago in 1910. A quote is inscribed on the photograph: "Sheep's plucks and bags, come awa," the words you would have heard being yelled by the meat market stallholders, as they tried to entice customers to buy the tasty ingredients for making haggis. Other references to the past are blue glazed bricks, like those seen in butcher shops, and paving striped like a butcher's apron.

This area was once the site of not just the meat market, but the cattle market and the municipal abattoir too. They were both relocated here in the mid-1800s in an attempt to clean up the Nor' Loch – the expanse of water that used to fill what is now Princes Street Gardens. The loch had become putrid with the effluent from the abattoir (not to mention a few human bodies: it was a popular site for body dumping and suicides).

Fountainbridge was chosen as the abattoir's new home since it was the terminus of the Union Canal – there was once a double basin here and you can see the route it took marked on the walkway leading east from the mural, with an underfoot installation of shining lights, each denoting a lock or bridge of the Glasgow to Edinburgh canal.

In the early 1900s the slaughterhouse and meat market moved again, this time much further out from the centre, to Chesser. In the 60s, the derelict market building was turned into the Americana discotheque, which then in the 80s became Chicago-themed club diner Fat Sam's, with the archway as its façade. Customers were watched over by a mannequin of the Fat Sam gangster, and a strange superstition arose that he must never leave or terrible things would occur. But worry not: you can still find him hidden in a cupboard at 1 Exchange Place. Anyone who crosses him will surely be dead meat …

CENTRAL HALL, TOLLCROSS

2 West Tollcross, Edinburgh EH3 9BP
• Tel: 0131 447 9787
• www.centralvenues.org
• Email: info@centralvenues.org
• Open Mon–Fri 9.30am–5pm, but closed if there's a booking or an event
• Admission free
• Buses: 2, 10, 11, 15, 16, 23, 27, 30, 45

Excess SS

I n 1948 the Cold War had iced over East-West relations and MI6 were in search of spies to slip through the Iron Curtain. They needed people who would look right, speak the language and carry off a decent accent. Who better than some Ukrainian prisoners of war they had kicking around in a northern Italian P.O.W. camp? Problem is, they were all SS soldiers, many of them high-ranking – but well, you know, my enemy's enemy …

MI6 brought the Ukrainians over, so they could be properly sorted into good spyage material and surplus SS. Put a thousand of them in a Nissen-hut camp on a golf course in Haddington, 30 km south of Edinburgh. And told everyone they were peaceful Ukrainians, here to help rebuild war-torn Britain.

As a front for these spy recruitment drives, MI6 set up a charity, the Scottish League for European Freedom (SLEF), purportedly to help impoverished refugees from Eastern Europe. They even appointed, as their chair, the unwitting Kitty Stewart-Murray, Duchess of Atholl, one of Britain's earliest female MPs, who was very outspoken in her anti-totalitarianism. In 1938 she had resigned her parliamentary seat in protest at Neville Chamberlain's policy of appeasement of Hitler. It was she who persuaded many of the Edinburgh "ladies who lunch" set to help raise funds for the charity.

One of the big events financed by the volunteers' coffee mornings and jumble sales was a conference at the beautiful 1901-built Central Hall in Tollcross, which has a huge auditorium, used for "cinematographic exhibitions" before Edinburgh had a picture house. Here, thought the members of the SLEF, downtrodden East Europeans would be able to voice their pleas for freedom. It was a great success – but unbeknown to the ladies, they had filled the grand venue with one of the biggest crowds of Nazis since Leni Riefenstahl filmed *Triumph of the Will*.

And yet all this subterfuge was in vain. Because at the time, Kim Philby was working at MI6 and passed on all the details to Moscow. Every time a Ukrainian spy was parachuted into enemy territory, they were immediately identified and shot. And the surplus SS in the Haddington camp? Well, it would have been churlish to expose the gullibility of their generous Scottish hosts just for the sake of a few war crime trials. So they just packed up the Nissen huts and let their former residents slip into the community …

See overleaf for traces of the city's old cinemas.

PHANTOMS OF THE CINEMA

Edinburgh has a proud cinematic history, with Edinburgh International Film Festival, the world's oldest continuously running film festival, based at the Filmhouse on Lothian Road. This is an ex-church, St Thomas's, turned cinema in 1979 – ironic as many of the city's old picture houses have converted the other way. If you're lucky, you might persuade someone at the Centre for the Moving Image to let you peer into the crypt under Cinema One, which must be haunted by the phantoms of many forgotten movies.

The first moving picture shown in Scotland was screened on Monday, 13 April 1896 (only a year after the Lumière brothers had patented their invention) at the Empire Palace of Varieties – now the location of Edinburgh Festival Theatre, where the E.I.F.F. holds its opening-night galas.

Edinburgh now has about ten cinemas, but many more have flickered in and out of existence. Over 120 are listed in George Baird's *Edinburgh Theatres, Cinemas and Circuses: 1820–1963*. Many of them opened in 1913, the boom year for cinema. Most have long since been demolished; even the ones that became bingo halls are starting to be replaced by luxury flats. But a few buildings still retain some afterglow of their cinematic origins. Here is a montage of edited highlights.

The Plaster Screen, 12 Casselbank Street, Edinburgh EH6 5HA

Before the advent of the talkies (which demanded that speakers be hidden behind the screen), silent movies were often projected onto plaster screens. The only one remaining in Scotland is in what is now the Destiny Church in Leith. It was built in 1885 as a Turkish bath – spot the Moorish clues like the onion-domed windows. It was converted into a cinema in 1920, though only for about ten years. Amazingly, the plaster screen remains intact, behind the makeshift stage.

The Waverley, 9 Infirmary Street, Edinburgh EH1 1NP

The single-storey stone outhouse of the former Lady Yester's Kirk was run until the early 1920s as a flea-ridden "penny scratcher" by a rag and bone man, who would also accept jam jars as payment from kids. Tickets often came with a free orange. In his excellent cinefile blog, "Shadow Play", David Cairns describes how "Happy young patrons could suck their orange while scratching themselves, making for a truly immersive and interactive experience."

The Haymarket Cinema, 90 Dalry Road, Edinburgh EH11 2AX

Until recently, you could still see the arched ceiling of Edinburgh's first purpose-built cinema, the Haymarket (later renamed the Scotia), which opened in 1912 and was run by John Maxwell. He went on to purchase Elstree Studios in London and to set up British International Pictures, for which he recruited little-known director Alfred Hitchcock. Together they made ten films, kicking off with *The Ring*; hitting success with one of the first British talkies, *Blackmail*; and drawing to a finale with *Number Seventeen*. The Scotia would draw in crowds to Hitchcock's movies until it closed in 1964.

The Tivoli, 52 Gorgie Road, Edinburgh EH11 2NB

Further down Dalry, you will see two Art Deco buildings that were built as cinemas. The Destiny Church occupies what was once the 1913-built Tivoli cinema. It was rebuilt in 1933 as the neon-fronted New Tivoli, which ran until 1973, having peaked with the ever-popular *Carry On* films. Inside, the Tiv had mood lighting, which could be matched to the movie. Smokey green for *Carry on Screaming*? Bathing-suit yellow for *Carry on Camping*?

Poole's Roxy, 392 Gorgie Road, Edinburgh EH11 2RN

At the far end of the same road is the glamorously-housed Bensons for Beds, originally the Roxy. Built in 1937, it attempted to outstrip the Tiv's lighting prowess with an iridescent neon tube bonanza worthy of Vegas. One of its patrons was the young John Lennon, accompanied by his Edinburgh cousin. The Poole family owners ran a chain of cinemas, including the Synod Hall on Castle Terrace (now the site of Saltire Court), where they screened their Myrioramas and Edinburgh's first talkie. Jim Poole went on to set up Edinburgh's first art house cinema, the Cameo.

The Princes Cinema, 131 Princes Street, Edinburgh EH2 4AH

If you stand with your back to the James Young Simpson statue and look up, you'll see wavy herringbone window frames of what seems to be an ornate conservatory plonked on top of the shops. This was the smoking lounge of the Princes Cinema, which opened in 1912, one of three cinemas on the street. The Princes screened shorts accompanied by a live orchestra, and you could walk in at any time. Perhaps due to orchestral exhaustion, in 1935 it became a news theatre, the Monseigneur, where they screened British Movietone and Pathé newsreels. In 1964 it regenerated as the Jacey, a "specialist" cinema, screening Chabrol's Lesbian romp, *Les Biches*, and closing in 1973 with a confused billing of *I Am Sexy* and *Do You Want to Remain a Virgin Forever?*

EAST

GHOST TREES OF LOCHEND PARK

Lochend Park, Lochend Road South, Edinburgh EH7 6DQ
- Tel: 0131 529 3111
- www.lochendpark.org
- Email: info@lochendpark.org
- Accessible 24 hrs
- Free
- Buses: 19, 34, 49

Not waving but drowning

Lochend Park is in a steep-sided dell, lined on each side by tall flats, a long wall and the towering Meadowbank stadium, so even when you pass by real close you can miss it. Many Restalrig locals don't realise it's there.

At the bottom of the dell is a small loch. And in the middle of the loch are some strange-looking trees. They seem to be some kind of mangrove-style swamp plant, their water-based roots transplanted from the Florida Keys. But they are actually drowning willows, submerged in the water that they once crowned.

The loch used to be much, much deeper, and there was an island in the middle. It is said that one moonless night, a coach and four accidentally drove into the water and disappeared without a trace. It was certainly quite dangerous: several people have drowned in its depths, the island acting as an irresistible lure to children.

The council decided something had to be done and tried to fill in the loch. But they overlooked the fact that it was fed from below by a spring, so it could never be filled. (Should have checked their old Scots dictionary: Restalrig means "ridge of swampland".) Willows like water, but not as much as this. Each spring they do a good impression of fighting back, but the truth is that they are losing the war. However, they do create a very unusual habitat – birds love the shaded, boggy site, with lots of nooks and crannies to investigate and shelter beneath.

On the side of the eastern slope is a 16th-century doocot (dovecote). During the 1645 outbreak of bubonic plague, it was converted into a plague kiln: the clothes and possessions of plague victims would be gathered and smoked in the kiln, then redistributed to the poor–- unfortunately still filled with their gently warmed, plague-carrying fleas. Over half the population of Leith and Edinburgh died.

But it's not all doom and gloom. This is a very beautiful park to wander round. On a sunny afternoon, the views from the doocot are fantastic. Former owner Sir Robert Logan of Restalrig would have known this. Unfortunately, he was on the wrong side in the Jacobite uprisings and he was allegedly involved in an attempt to abduct James VI, the so-called "Gowrie conspiracy". Logan was already dead, but he was tried – as a corpse – and found guilty of treason. His lands and his possessions were confiscated from his family, who were made homeless. Which is why you can now enjoy the park as a public space. Happy days.

ST TRIDUANA'S CHAPEL

St Margaret's parish church
176 Restalrig Road South, Edinburgh EH7 6EA
• Tel: 0131 554 7400
• Email: stmpc@btconnect.com
• Tours by appointment only
• Buses: 19, 21 25, 34, 42, 49

*A sight
for sore eyes*

Just off the roundabout at the bottom of the hill from Jock's Lodge, St Margaret's is a small village church with a very pretty graveyard and a small chapel outside. This is all that is left of what was once a huge collegiate foundation called Restalrig which, in 1560, was one of the locations noted on the maps of the Seige of Leith. Back then it had thirty-two altars, a two-storey King's Chapel, eight canons, two singing boys and a Dean who later presided over the marriage of Mary Queen of Scots and Lord Darnley. However, when John Knox started his Reformation, one of the earliest acts of the first General Assembly of the Church of Scotland decreed that "as a monument of idolatrie, Restalrig should be utterly casten downe and destroyit". The great foundation was reduced to a single nave and a pile of rubble, which was soon covered over by a grassy mound.

In 1907 gardeners discovered that the grassy mound contained the still intact undercroft of the King's Chapel. This unusual hexagonal chapel, which was built between 1477 and 1515 and may have been modelled on one in Jerusalem, was excavated and sensitively restored by Thomas Ross. The name Restalrig means miry or boggy field, and the source of the saturation lay inside.

Below the chapel is an ancient spring, dedicated to St Triduana. Pilgrims used to come here to bathe their eyes, believing the waters would restore their sight. According to legend, the beautiful and virginal Triduana was being courted by Nectan, the King of the Picts, whose advances she was attempting to fend off. She asked him what it was about her he found so attractive, and Nectan claimed it was her lovely eyes. So she promptly gouged out her eyeballs with a thorny stick, and sent them to him. An act which apparently impressed him greatly.

You can see St Triduana posing with her weapon of choice, high on the chapel wall. A pump runs twenty-four hours a day to keep the spring from springing, otherwise it would turn the subterranean chapel into a large paddling pool. There is a ledge all round the edge and the floor is made of stone flags, so it seems rather made for it. But if you want to see the balm well, you have to lift a heavy slab away from this ledge and peer down into the murky depths. If truth be told, it doesn't look like the most sanitary eye bath. But who know what powers it possesses …?

MEADOWBANK VELODROME

London Road, Edinburgh EH7 6AE
• www.edinburghrc.co.uk
• Email via contact page on website
• Opening hours info on website. Closed in winter
• Taster session: £10 for an hour, including bike hire and British Cycling accredited coaching. Spectators free
• Buses: 4, 5, 15, 26, 44, 45, 104, 113

Back pedalling

You don't need to be a cycling enthusiast to love this beautiful, fading cycle race track – though it's mainly only serious cyclists who know about this velodrome, built almost fifty years ago for the 1970 Commonwealth Games. Now its days are numbered – it's been threatened with demolition for years as part of the redevelopment of the entire Meadowbank Sports Centre, but each year it somehow manages to escape execution. This is where Sir Chris Hoy trained and he is among those campaigning to keep the place open. Move fast and you might just get there before it disappears for ever. It tends to be open in late spring after an inspection, and on track days you can come and watch lycra-clad action.

Walking into the velodrome is like entering a secret world. You head into the sports centre car park and walk east, where you will find an old path that follows the line of the train track, shadowed to your right by the huge edifice that is St Margaret's House – an ex-government building converted into fantastic artists' studios: Edinburgh Palette (well worth a visit). At the end, you will see the façade of an oval structure, covered in amazing graffiti created by some of the Palette people. Enter the dangerous-looking tunnel below and emerge into the centre of a thing of beauty: a banked cycle racing track made out of the finest wooden boards, with thin blue and red lines tracing the curves, and a grassy central viewing lawn at the base.

Unlike most modern stadiums, this track is open to the elements and the views around are fantastic. If you visit when the track is unused, you can walk up the surprisingly steep bank and see the rows of Edinburgh tenements spreading out below, Arthur's Seat rising above. The morning light glints across the boards and, even with no one on it, the track seems to emanate a sense of speed.

Sadly, the very fact that it is open air is the root of its obsolescence. It costs a fortune to keep the track safe from warping wood and crumbling support struts. Soon it will be replaced by a modern track, but until then, this is a space to set your wheels in a spin.

NEARBY

Just by the stadium is a large menhir marking the St Margaret's Well, once a site of 15th-century Restalrig pilgrimage. Due to the building of a new train depot in 1859, the stone edifice was moved to the Queen's Park, Holyrood, and can still be found there, now sitting over St David's Well.

MUSCHET'S CAIRN

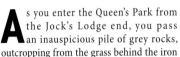

4

Duke's Walk, Queen's Park, Edinburgh EH8 8JB
• Viewable 24 hrs
• Free
• Buses: 4, 5, 15, 26, 44, 45, 104, 113

*Five times
a murder*

As you enter the Queen's Park from the Jock's Lodge end, you pass an inauspicious pile of grey rocks, outcropping from the grass behind the iron railings to the right. There's no sign to show that this is a site of any interest, but the heap of stones commemorates the horrible murder of 16-year-old Margaret Hall by her husband, Nicol Muschet, on 17 October 1720.

Muschet had met Margaret just over a year earlier and married her only three weeks later. In his lengthy defence, he claimed that she forced herself upon him, that he never loved her and that her family had designs upon his money. So, poor defenceless victim, he did what anyone would do in such a predicament – plot ways to get rid of her without payout.

Plot 1. Defamation - Muschet would pay his friend James Campbell to produce testimonies of Margaret's "whorish practices" and also drug the girl with laudanum and have her raped by an obliging professor pal. But the lawyer who drew up their contract pointed out that Margaret's "infidelity" with the professor wouldn't stand up in a court of law if no prior acquaintance could be proved.

Plot 2. Poison - Muschet paid his cousin - also a James - to give Margaret a dose of poison, which he disguised in a dram of whisky. Margaret became very sick, but did not die. Several more drams were administered but she still stubbornly refused to expire.

Plot 3. Drowning - Cousin James' wife Grissel suggested that her husband take Margaret out riding on the back of his horse and, when they were passing a river, shove her in. But James Campbell thought it too shaky. How about pushing her "into some Hole without the Town, and immediately thereafter to flee to Paris"? Cousin James refused to take such a risk.

Plot 4. Bludgeoning - Grissel would entertain Margaret for the evening and then, as she walked home, Cousin James would spring out on her, armed with a heavy weapon. They made several attempts, but every time someone was passing, and James had to melt back into the shadows.

Plot 5. Stabbing - Finally, Muschet decided to take matters into his own hands. He took Margaret for an after-dark walk where, sensing that he was up to something, she began to weep. He attacked her with a knife, with some difficulty, and finally managed to stab her to death. They had been married just over a year.

But unsurprisingly there was a flaw in this perfect plan – Muschet had left his monogrammed shirt at the crime scene, which led officers to question his family. Grissel quickly confessed. And just as quickly Muschet was found guilty and hanged. Once only.

THOMSON'S TOWER

Dr Neil's Garden, Old Church Lane, Duddingston Village, Edinburgh EH15 3PX
• Tel: 07849 187 995
• www.drneilsgarden.co.uk
• Email: info@drneilsgarden.co.uk
• Open Sun 2pm–4pm during July and August, or by special arrangement

Slip-slidin' away

Winters in the 18th century were much harsher than those the current residents of Edinburgh are used to. Back then, the expanse of water which covered Princes Street Gardens – the Nor' Loch – could be counted on to freeze over, and ice skating and curling became very popular sports. But in 1813 the loch was drained and the centre of the winter social sports scene switched to Duddingston Loch.

A huge number of people would gather here on the ice – you can see them in old photos, postcards and paintings. Charles Altamont Doyle, Arthur Conan Doyle's father, painted many scenes of Duddingston Loch ice sports. Raeburn painted his famous *Skating Minister* here.

With all this activity, the Duddingston Curling Society decided they needed a proper curling house and commissioned William Playfair to design it. The octagonal tower he built them had a loch-level floor to house the stones and an upper floor to warm up in and watch the games. The Rev. Thomson, after whom the tower is named, also used it as his painting studio as it had views over the loch envied by Turner himself.

The rules of modern curling are based on those drawn up here to avoid fighting on the ice floor. They included fines for "uttering oaths and introducing a political subject into conversation". The Curling Society shared a safety officer with the Ice Skating Society; his specialist safety equipment consisted of ropes and a long ladder.

The tower still stands in the rather secret Dr Neil's Garden, created in the 1960s by husband and wife doctors, Andrew and Nancy Neil. Wander down through their beautifully planted terraced slopes and at the water's edge you'll find the tower.

The top floor, with its beautiful views, can be hired for private events and the lower floor is now a museum of curling. Around the base of the walls are old curling stones ranging from found lumps of rock to specially polished and handled ones made from the Blue Hone granite found only on Ailsa Craig – prized due to its very low water absorption, which prevents corrosive ice crystals from getting in. You can watch an old film of the lumps of quarried stone being thrown into a rather unstable-looking boat. On the walls are reproductions of the aforementioned paintings and photos, among them a hanging pair of old curling shoes: one sole grippy, the other smooth.

DUDDINGSTON FIELD

Entrance through gate between 56 & 58 The Causeway, Duddingston Village, Edinburgh EH15 3QA
- Always open (gates are shut but not locked 4pm–10am)
- Admission free
- www.duddingstonfield.org.uk
- Email: secretary@duddingstonfield.com
- Bus: 42

> *A hidden labyrinth on Arthur's Seat*

Just across from the Sheep Heid Inn in Duddingston Village is a wrought-iron gate which opens onto an old brick pathway. This leads up between the houses and into a hidden Duddingston community world, spread across the lower slopes of Dunsapie Hill – the back haunches of the resting lion that is Arthur's Seat. Much of the land used to belong to the McEwan brewing family, who lived next door in Bellavista House. On your right is what was once their tennis courts, now a large grassy space with picnic benches sheltered from the summer heat by great lime and ash trees, with a fire pit to warm against the autumn chill and accompany the local fireworks on Bonfire Night.

The path leads on up to the next terrace – passing sheds, greenhouses and compost bins. Go through the wooden gate and you are now in the field itself. This was a grassland area grazed for decades by horses until the council raised the rent and then decided to sell it. A group of local volunteers raised enough funds to save it from being developed for housing, with the promise that it would be used for public access and the preservation of wildlife.

As you enter the field, you are greeted by a clutch of handsome chickens, crowding round to see if you've brought them any tasty morsels. Behind them, a sapling orchard planted in 2012 promises a future bite of each of the forty-eight native Scottish varieties of apple. As the hill opens out, you are at the start of a measured walk around the field. It's a steep incline and it gets pretty muddy after rain, but every 600 metres or so there's a bench to rest on, re-gather your energy and set off again. It's perfect for anyone who likes a bit of an incentive to keep going. From each target bench you are rewarded with a different view to admire: Duddingston Loch, Craigmillar Castle, the Firth of Forth, the Pentland Hills … and all the while, Arthur's Seat towering above.

But look more closely and half-way up the hill you will spot a labyrinth cut into the grass: follow this elaborately twisting pathway to its centre and contemplate the idea of creativity, journeys, origins and the interior. At the top of the field is the "nick in the wall", a stile in the ancient stone boundary, which leads to a hidden route up to Dunsapie Loch, and over onto the magnificence of Arthur's Seat.

"CHILDREN AT PLAY" MURAL

John Maxwell Gallery, Space, 11 Harewood Road, Edinburgh EH16 4NT
• Tel: 0131 659 4759
• www.lyratheatre.co.uk
• Email: jo@lyratheatre.co.uk
• Admission times and prices vary
• Buses: 2, 14, 21, 30

Recurring dreamscape

The old 1930s Craigmillar school building has been converted into a large Social Enterprise Complex called "Space". It houses many organisations, along with an art gallery and a community theatre, which have changing exhibitions and performances aimed at children.

But hidden behind whatever elaborate set has been constructed, you will find the wonderful "Children at Play" mural by celebrated Scottish artist John Maxwell, who gave his name to the gallery. Conjuring up a dream of playground and community happiness, the mural was painted in the 1930s, when the building opened as a primary school. It had been badly damaged by time and neglect, but was rediscovered and restored when the building became a community hub.

Maxwell trained under Fernand Léger alongside Marc Chagall and there's something Chagallian in the floating imaginary landscape, though this one is filled mainly with happy skipping schoolkids and fewer violin-playing goats. It's a pity that it gets so frequently covered up and is hard to access, especially since it was the preservation of this painting that saved the school from being knocked down. But maybe it is like a recurring dream, destined to be perpetually rediscovered by each new generation.

NEARBY

"HERE": THE HAY CHAIR
Junction of Niddrie Mains Road and Hay Avenue, Edinburgh EH16 4AQ

A giant grey granite chair sits by the roundabout at the foot of Hay Avenue. Sitting on the giant chair is a tiny brown chair. Designed by Doug Cocker, it was installed in 2004. It references the seat of King Arthur, or the high hopes for the regeneration of Craigmillar, or, to paraphrase Sir Isaac Newton, the wee man sitting on the big man's shoulders. Whether Edinburgh or Craigmillar is the big man is the subject of debate. The larger chair also forms the letter H, for Hay Avenue and for Here, in celebration of the redevelopment of the area, as here is the place to be.

The choice of grey makes the chair disappear on overcast days and the seams of the tiles have let in water, which gives it a patchy effect, unfortunately conjuring up memories of badly constructed housing. But when you get up close, you discover something hidden on its inside leg. Inscribed on the highly polished surface are drawings by local schoolchildren, twenty of them, with the child's name below: Brogan, Samantha, Chentelle, Michelle et al., who must be young adults now, sitting on a chair somewhere, remembering their Craigmillar childhood.

HELEN CRUMMY SCULPTURE

Outside Craigmillar Library
101 Niddrie Mains Rd, Edinburgh EH16 4DS
• Viewable 24 hrs
• Admission free
• Buses: 2, 14, 21, 30

*Fiddler
in the sun*

I t is a peculiar MacFact that despite the minimal quotas of sunshine, Scotland has more Renaissance sundials than any other country. Not only were they the perfect intersection between art and science, they also chime with the Presbyterian requirement that if you're going to create something as extravagant as a sculpture, it had better do something useful. No square of lawn was complete without a shadow-casting plinth, preferably with a suitable inscription to remind you of the transitory nature of life and the imminence of death. *Tempus fugit. Carpe diem. Memor esto brevis ævi.*

But artist Tim Chalk sees sundials in Scotland as a statement of optimism, a defiant belief that the sun will shine. In Craigmillar, he has taken this art of the elongated shadow to new lengths. His sculpture of Helen Crummy MBE, the world-renowned social activist who set up the Craigmillar Festival to celebrate local talent, is also a giant sundial. The group who commissioned the piece had quite a tight brief: a depiction of Helen giving her young son Philip a violin – related to the story of her being spurred into action after asking the headmaster if Philip could have violin lessons and being told it wasn't possible. Her reaction not only ensured music and art lessons for the local children, but also galvanised and transformed the community. With the local school gone, the rebuilding of Craigmillar stalled and arts funding at a low, Helen Crummy's determined spirit is much needed.

Chalk extended his brief to reflect these values – he placed the sculpture on a low plinth so that children can climb on it rather than view it reverentially. He set the bronze cast figures inside a symbolic open doorway, decorated with panels created by the young and old of the local community. One pictures Jimmy Boyle's sadly demolished Gulliver sculpture, which used to lie in the fields nearby. Another shows a child sitting at a PC in the new library.

And the dialling of the sun? Well, the violin is the gnomon, the shadow-casting part. On the ground is a predictive outline of the silhouette which is formed every year at noon on 17 September, commemorating the unveiling, in 1930, of the first house in the original Craigmillar scheme. Unfortunately, the first two anniversaries since the sculpture was unveiled were clouded over but Craigmillar can be sure that the sun will return: *Sol omnibus lucet.*

THE WHITE HOUSE

70 Niddrie Mains Road, Edinburgh EH16 4BG
- Tel: 0131 468 1934
- www.thewhitehousekitchen.org.uk
- Email: info@thewhitehousekitchen.org.uk
- Open Mon–Fri 8am–4pm: admission free. Also open for special events: see website for prices
- Buses: 2, 14, 21, 30

There are only a few Art Deco buildings left in Edinburgh: St Andrew's House (see p. 91), the Maybury Casino, the Causewayside garage (see below) and The White House in Craigmillar. Other beautiful pieces of early modernist design, like the Hillburn at Fairmilehead, have been tragically demolished. But despite drifting perilously close to this precipice, happily The White House has surged back.

One of Edinburgh's few remaining Art Deco buildings

Designed by William Innes Thomson in 1936, like the Maybury and the Hillburn, The White House was originally built as a roadhouse – a glamorous venue for motorists to stop and rest, at a time when cars were an exciting new luxury and driving was akin to taking a cruise. The White House was transatlantic ship shaped – on board were a bar, a tearoom, a skittle alley and a billiard room.

As motoring lost its glamour, The White House became a pub and then slowly disintegrated until all but one room was condemned – not that it dampened the thirst of the regulars, who apparently used to get through two lorry loads of booze a week. The pub finally closed in 2001 and then lay empty for six years, reaching the Buildings at Risk Register.

Thankfully it was bought up by local regenerators PARC: the Art Deco interiors were authentically recreated, using the original linen printed designs found in the City Council's archive. Today, the ground floor houses an exhibition space and a community café that grows its own produce in raised beds in the back garden. The Red Room hosts music gigs, screenings, tea dances and even sing-alongs for those who might remember the days of the old roadhouse.

NEARBY

SOUTHERN MOTORS GARAGE

39 Causewayside, Edinburgh EH9 1QF

If you are keen to see more Art Deco, drive down to Causewayside and drop in at the Majestic wine warehouse. Overhead is the structure of the beautiful Southern Motors Garage, complete with elegant wide windows and vertical In and Out signage. It was designed in 1933 by the 26-year-old recent graduate of Edinburgh College of Art, Sir Basil Spence. Now a private residence, the garage stopped trading in the 1990s and the building would have been demolished had there not been a determined defence mounted by architects, keen to save not just a beautiful building but one of Spence's earliest commissions.

WAUCHOPE MAUSOLEUM

Alley between 34 and 36 Niddrie House Drive, Edinburgh EH16 4UP
• Open during Doors Open Day (Sept.), or on rare occasions by appointment
• Email: eastteam@edinburgh.gov.uk
• Buses: 2, 21, 30

*A tomb
in hiding*

The Wauchope Mausoleum has got to win the grand prize in the game of neoclassical monument hide and seek. Even if you find the right street in the middle of the unlikely Niddrie Estate, you still can't see it because it's entirely sardined between blocks of 1970s harled concrete flats. And then your way through is barred by rusty iron gates. Apart from rarely granted requests, it's only really open to the public on Doors Open Day, its dim interior walls illuminated by flickering candlelight.

A classically styled stone chamber built in 1735, it's the last remnants of the Wauchopes (pronounced with a soft central *ch*, as in *loch*), who owned this area for over 600 years. Their HQ was a very grand towered house, Niddrie Marischal, with a chapel in its grounds. Over the doorway of the mausoleum is the adage *PARTA TUERE*: "Defend what you have earned." But over the years, this has proved a rather tricky family motto to adhere to.

In 1597 the then owner Archibald Wauchope, who had been imprisoned for several murders and an attempt to assassinate James VI, was, for the second time, attempting to escape from a window when he fell and broke his neck. Feeling this was not punishment enough, his estate was confiscated and his castle burned down by an angry mob.

Francis Wauchope managed to regain the estate by marrying the new owner's daughter. In 1636 the house was rebuilt from the ruins. But in 1687 another angry mob, this time set against Jesuits, burned down the chapel. Forty-eight years later, Andrew Wauchope built this mausoleum over the burial slab of his ancestor William, using stones from the original chapel. When his wife died in 1780, he added a lengthy memorial on the back wall, cataloguing her qualities: "a virtuous affectionate and complacent wife", "mild benevolent social and cheerful without artifice", whose body was "well formed and agreeable" and after bearing him thirteen children, "calmly quitted her mortal frame without emotion or complaint".

Despite all these offspring, the Wauchope line eventually died out in 1943, and the increasingly derelict house and the lands were sold to Edinburgh City Council. In 1959 the *Evening News* Hogmanay headline was "Edinburgh Mansion House Gutted by a Spectacular Fire", allowing it to be demolished in 1971 to make way for the new housing estate. Perhaps hiding here is a lonely mausoleum's only form of defence.

CRAIGMILLAR CASTLE

Craigmillar Castle Road, Edinburgh EH16 4SY
• Tel: 0131 661 4445
• www.historic-scotland.gov.uk/craigmillarcastle
• For junior guide tours, email: jade.somerville@scotland.gsi.gov.uk
• Open 1 April–30 Sept: Mon–Sun, 9.30am–5.30pm. 1 Oct–31 March:
Mon, Tues, Wed, Sat & Sun 10am–4pm. Closed 25 & 26 Dec and 1 & 2 Jan
Adult £5.50; child £3.30; concession £4.40
• Buses: 7, 8, 18, 21, 24, 33, 38, 49

*Turrets
syndrome*

People vaguely know about Craigmillar Castle but most don't get round to visiting. And yet it is Scotland's most perfectly preserved medieval castle, surrounded by high curtain walls, towering to four floors, joined by numerous Escher-like twisting stairwells. What is it that makes the footfall so faint? Is a visit to the endless winds of Edinburgh Castle so totally exhausting that by the end of the seventeenth circle, folk are just all castled out?

Craigmillar Castle is so much more liberating – there's space, quiet, and much less gift shoppage. You can explore it freestyle, at your own pace and route, or you can get taken on a dramatised tour by children from the local Castleview Primary: 10- and 11-year-olds, performing in character, dressed in full period costume, all experts in the history of this building, which has seen countless real-life dramas unfold – most infamously, that of frequent visitor Mary Queen of Scots.

Let your diminutive hosts, small Sir Simon Preston and his wife, little Lady Elizabeth, show you round their 14th-century abode, accompanied by their Lilliputian servants. They will tell you about their famous guests, show you round the cooking facilities, and point out the wall where a bricked-in skeleton was found, probably alive at the time of the ghoulish DIY project.

They will also point out the trace of a P-shaped pond on the back lawns – P for Prestwick. That's not the only (slightly egotistical) insignia – carved on one of the walls is a heraldic stone plaque featuring a wine press and a barrel, or tun: Preston. Get it? A terrible pun. Don't get that in your official full-sized Edinburgh Castle tour now, do you?

NEARBY

The area where the Royal Infirmary is located is known as Little France because Mary's French retinue stayed there when she visited Craigmillar. In 2010 J.K. Rowling funded the building of a regenerative neurology clinic and research centre in the grounds, named after her mother, Anne Rowling, who died of multiple sclerosis, aged only 45. The low grey and cream futuristic building (49 Little France Crescent, Edinburgh EH16 4SB) is interesting to see from the outside, and you can go inside and explore each September on Doors Open Day.

DOUBLE GRAVE OF BEAUTY AND THE GREAT LAFAYETTE ⑫

Piershill cemetery
Tall white gravestone at top of mound, just inside entrance from Piersfield Terrace
204 Piersfield Terrace, Edinburgh EH8 7BN
• Open dawn to dusk
• Admission free
• Buses: 15, 26, 45, 69

For never was a story of more woe. Than this of Beauty and her Romeo

He was Sigmund Neuberger, aka "the Great Lafayette", the most famous magician of his time. She was Beauty, a crossbred terrier puppy given to him by Harry Houdini. She was his Juliet. He was her provider of five-course meals, diamond-studded collars and her own suite of rooms with miniature dog furniture. A plaque over the door of his London home read, "The more I see of men the more I love my dog." But Lafayette loved Beauty so much he literally fed her to death. She died of apoplexy – a stroke brought on by overfeeding – four days before he was due to open his much-publicised run at Edinburgh's Empire Theatre of Varieties (now the Festival Theatre).

It was May 1911. Lafayette was devastated. He fought Edinburgh City Council for Beauty to be allowed to be buried like a human, a wish that could be granted if he agreed to share the plot at Piershill cemetery when his time came …

It was the night before Beauty's funeral and the Empire Theatre was packed. The GrLft's spectacular show was almost at an end. He had changed his flamboyant costumes a dozen times. He had shaken a flock of birds and a goat from a sequined cloth. And now he began his finale, "The Lion's Bride". Jugglers juggled, fire-eaters smouldered, a stallion reared and a helpless maiden was trapped in a cage with a furious lion – which dropped its pelt to reveal it was the Great Lafayette!

But a faulty lamp ignited the set. The audience calmly watched the fire spread, assuming it was part of the show. The only way to get them moving was for the orchestra to strike up a verse of "God Save the King". The safety curtain went down and jammed stuck, trapping the performers on stage and creating a perfect air suction to whip the flames into an inferno. The side doors had been locked by Lafayette to prevent snoopers discovering his trade secrets.

The GrLft made it out alive but then, demented, went back inside to save his horse. His body and that of ten of his company were found among the ashes of the building. But two days later, another Lafayette body was discovered, this one with his signature rings. It turned out that the first one was his secret body double. Some 250,000 people turned out for his funeral and watched the (correct) ashes being driven in a gilded carriage through the streets of Edinburgh, to be buried between the embalmed paws of his beloved pet.

See overleaf for more of Edinburgh's treasured pooches.

CAPITAL CANINES

Toby: 12-13 St Andrew Square, Edinburgh EH2 2AF
Bum: 36 King's Stables Rd, Edinburgh EH1 2EU
Cuillin: Colinton Parish Church Dell Rd, Edinburgh EH13 0JR
Dobbler: Cemetery for Soldiers' Dogs, Edinburgh Castle, Castlehill, Edinburgh EH1 2NG
Maida: Scott monument, East Princes St Gardens, Edinburgh EH2 2EJ

Greyfriars Bobby may be Edinburgh's most legendary canine, but there are other dogs who have had greater days: wee Bobby has lately been exposed as a Victorian PR stunt, conjured up by the cemetery's tour guide and a local restaurateur. They encouraged a stray mongrel to stay by feeding him and even replaced him with a lookalikie when their cash-dog inconveniently died.

James Clerk Maxwell loved animals – found them easier to get on with than humans. His Irish Terrier dog, Toby, rests beneath his feet in Alexander Stoddart's sculpture of the eminent physicist on George Street. This is near the house in India Street where he lived and which houses a small Maxwell museum (see p. 69). Maxwell used to explain his theories to Toby and examine his eyes with a homemade ophthalmoscope to try and understand colour blindness. Look carefully and you will see, just above Toby's head, some missing rivets in the chair upholstery: this demonstrates the second law of thermodynamics, which is, as Toby would have known, that things fall apart (especially when chewed).

Inside the King's Stables Road entrance to Princes Street Gardens hides a statue of a three-legged St Bernard–Spaniel cross called Bum. Like the real Greyfriars Bobby, he was a vagrant who in the late 1800s wandered the streets, not of Edinburgh, but of her twin city, San Diego, where Bobby and Bum's statues are proudly mounted side by side. Legend has it that Bum lost his leg in a daring railway-track rescue of a puppy, though it was probably during a fight with a Bulldog. He became so well known that San Diego adopted him as their unofficial mascot, awarded him the special order of a Tag for Life for PR services to the city, and stamped his picture on their dog licences. Bum lived out his days being fed by the top restaurants (signs in their windows proudly declared, "Bum eats here") and giving children rides on his back, though he developed a penchant for hard liquor, perhaps to numb the pain or humiliation.

Pain numbing was the speciality of another Edinburgh pooch belonging to James Young Simpson, the obstetrician who discovered the anaesthetic properties of chloroform and got the royal seal of approval from Queen Victoria when she gave birth to her ninth child. Simpson famously researched the pain-killing properties of various preparations with his colleagues by playing an inhalation version of Russian roulette. Luckily, chloroform was discovered to be a knock-out before anyone actually died. Simpson subsequently tested the dosage out on his faithful Boxer – his statue, sadly hidden from the public, sits by the front door of the privately owned Strathavon Lodge on Laverockbank Road.

More visible, but equally hidden away (in a corner of Edinburgh Castle), is the Cemetery for Soldiers' Dogs. It's a little walled garden just above where the 1 o'clock gun is fired – although it can only be viewed from above, you can make out the headstones. Faithful residents include Dobbler, who was buried here in 1893 after having trekked across half of Asia and Africa with the Argyll and Sutherland Highlanders.

The Great Lafayette evidently thought that Beauty (see p. 233) should live for ever. Robert Louis Stevenson clearly agreed as he wrote, "You think dogs will not be in heaven? I tell you, they will be there long before any of us." His own pet Skye Terrier, Cuillin, is commemorated in a bronze statue of Stevenson as a young boy outside Colinton Parish Church, where he used to visit his grandfather, a minister there.

Sir Walter Scott was another great literary lover of dogs, and they frequently appear in portraits of the writer. There is even a breed of dog, Dandie Dinmont Terriers, named after a character that appears in Scott's novel, *Guy Mannering*. You can see Scott's favourite dog, Maida, a wolf and Deerhound cross, curling at the foot of the Scott Monument statue. She was named after the Napoleonic battle of Maida because she was given to Scott by Alexander Macdonell, whose brother led the 78th Highlanders to victory there against the French.

When Maida finally passed away aged 8, Scott was devastated – he had a statue of her (beneath which she was interred) erected at Abbotsford House in the Borders. Scott wrote, "The misery of keeping a dog is his dying so soon. But, to be sure, if he lived for fifty years and then died, what would become of me?"

CRAIGENTINNY MARBLES ⓭

3c Craigentinny Crescent, Edinburgh EH7 6PR
• Viewable from road 24 hrs
• Admission free
• Buses: 15, 21, 26, 45, 69

A Roman mausoleum in a housing suburb

The Craigentinny estate is largely made up of 1930s pebble-dash bungalows, spreading down the hill towards the Firth from Moira Terrace. But as you cross the brow of Craigentinny Crescent, you are suddenly confronted by something totally alien that seems to have crash-landed in the estate's backyard. An enormous neoclassical mausoleum towers over the surrounding houses and bowling green, with the most exquisite white carved panels on each side. It's more like something you would find on Rome's Appian Way than in an Edinburgh housing suburb.

Here lies William Henry Miller, a rather eccentric gentleman, MP for Newcastle-under-Lyme, antiquarian and reclusive bachelor, who inherited the land here along with Craigentinny Castle. His peculiarities included an OCD-

style obsession with collecting and measuring books. When he died in 1848, wealthy and without an heir, he left £20,000 for something to be erected to commemorate his life and celebrate the arts. It was to be sited in what were then open fields at Craigentinny – and not in a churchyard.

The architect David Rhind designed the mausoleum and one of the finest British sculptors of the time, Alfred Gatley, was commissioned to create the bas-relief carvings. On the south side, Gatley depicts Moses and the Israelites crossing the Red Sea, holding aloft their prized possessions (an amphora and, oddly, a couple of tambourines) and dragging their cattle, two camels and a goat. Their figures are draped in the most delicately carved cloth; it seems to genuinely float over their limbs. On the north side, Pharaoh and his strapping Egyptian army charge after them into the rising sea, plunging to their deaths as the closing waves envelop their chariots, the warriors trampled underhoof by tumbling horses.

Miller's body is buried, according to his wishes, 40 feet below – down a stone-lined shaft with a heavy slab over his coffin. There were rumours that this was because he was trying to protect the secret of his sexual identity, that he was perhaps a changeling or even a woman who had masqueraded as a man. It's more likely that he, like the Pharoahs, was excessively paranoid about grave robbers: Burke and Hare were around when he was growing up. And there's nothing like a 50-foot monument to keep things discreet …

PORTOBELLO BOTTLE KILNS

25 Bridge Street, Portobello, Edinburgh EH15 1TG
• www.portobelloheritagetrust.co.uk
• Viewable from outside 24 hrs
• Free
• Buses: 15, 21, 26, 40, 42, 45, 49, 104

*Curvaceous
kilns*

Scotland's last two surviving bottle kilns are not visible from Portobello High Street, but you can see their wide brick funnels peeking over the tops of the houses as you walk along the promenade. Twelve metres high, widening to a 7-metre diameter at the base, their voluptuous brick curves are braced by a corset of iron strips (*bonts*) to strengthen them as they expanded during firing.

The Rubenesque twins are now entirely enveloped by the hard modern lines of the new Harbour Green estate. But this area used to be the centre of a major Scottish industry: pottery production. From the late 1700s, there were potteries all along the coast from Bo'ness to Cockenzie, employing several thousand workers. These two kilns, built in 1906 and 1909, were part of Buchan's Pottery (A.W. Buchan & Co), which originally specialised in making utilitarian stoneware containers – ginger beer bottles, whisky flagons, bed warmers. After the Second World War, they moved into more refined tableware, with thistle and floral patterns on white glaze. You'll find a collection of Buchanware in the Museum of Edinburgh and pictures on the Portobello Heritage Trust website.

There were originally three bottle kilns, working in rotation – one stacking, one firing and one emptying. With ten coal fires stoked in a pit below the main chamber, temperatures inside could reach 1300°C. The ingenious design has an inner chamber around which the hot air can circulate as well as being drawn up through the middle. The firing chamber would be filled with close-stacked towers of clay boxes (*saggars*), each containing a different pot, allowing hundreds to be fired in one go.

In the mid-fifties Buchan's moved to electric kilns and finally closed the site down in 1970. The disused bottle kilns gradually became colonised by nature and served as rather grand doo'cots – local kids would gather pigeon eggs from inside. They were on the verge of collapse when they were rescued by the Portobello Heritage Trust, which petitioned Edinburgh Council to restore them. Sadly, the council tried to cut corners by just repointing the bricks, whereupon the chimney of the west kiln simply crumbled. The top section had to be rebuilt, this time by specialists who had worked in the potteries in Stoke-upon-Trent. The placing of the final brick was celebrated with a grand topping-out ceremony in November 2013 and now, thankfully, our beautiful broads are safe.

COADE STONE PILLARS

Portobello Community Garden, John Street, Portobello, Edinburgh EH15 2EB
• Accessible 24 hrs
• Free
• Buses: 15, 26, 40, 45

Pillars of the community

Just back from the Portobello seafront are three elegantly decorated columns, looking for all the world like they are holding up an invisible temple, or perhaps ready to carry out some architectural variation on the Indian rope trick. They are in fact a monument to the power of the local community, who struggled for thirty years to preserve this beautiful folly *à trois*.

The columns originally stood on the other side of Portobello in the grounds of Argyle House on Hope Lane. In the mid-1980s the house was being demolished for redevelopment by Edinburgh Council, which somehow managed to forget that the columns were grade 2 listed. John Stewart and the Portobello Amenity Society (PAS) stood in front of the bulldozers and managed to save the beloved pillars from the rubble heap, despite not really knowing what they were or having anywhere to put them.

For decades, the disassembled blocks rested in council storage while the society fought to raise the funds to have them restored and relocated. In her research, PAS member Celia Butterworth found that the columns had exactly the same Tudor rose, fleur-de-lys and lion-with-primrose patterns as the chimneys (built in 1814) at Dalmeny House – the Dalmeny family name being Primrose. Whether the columns were spares, seconds or what John Stewart terms "felaffas" ("felaffa the back of a lorry"), no one is sure.

Although the columns seem to be ornately carved out of stone, they are actually made of Coade stone, an artificial mix which is as strong and durable as stone, but can be moulded and fired like pottery. This ingenious concoction was developed in 1770 by one Mrs Eleanor Coade, a businesswoman who catered to a roaring trade in Victorians returning from their Grand Tours and who fancied a piece of classical garden ornamentation.

The Coade stone on these columns had been buried under layers of paint, which Graciela Ainsworth and her renowned team of stone conservators carefully cleaned off. They then reconstructed this giant 3D jigsaw with new steel internal support, though some bits were missing. The Coade-stone recipe had long been lost, but after much trial and error, local potter Alison Robinson managed to recreate the mix and make new capitals for the top of two of the pillars. And finally a suitable location was found, on the site of a derelict paddling pool. All in all, a towering achievement.

See overleaf for more about Coade stone.

CRACKING THE COADE

Coade stone, or *Lithodipyra,* is an ingenious substance – a ceramic which resembles stone and fires equally hard, so it can be used to produce statues, architectural decorations and garden ornaments. These can be cast in moulds, allowing very fine detail and exact replication.

Lithodipyra means "twice-fired stone" because the mix contains finely ground fired clay or "grog". The colour of the resulting artificial stone changed, depending on the grog, so pieces could be made to match all different types of rock, from red sandstone to white marble. Coade stone doesn't shrink and is incredibly durable, often surviving the elements far longer than actual carved stone. This explains why it became very popular among owners of stately homes in search of a showy ornamental statement, and with eminent architects looking to embellish their buildings, especially Robert Adam, John Nash and John Soane.

The woman who perfected this recipe and firing technique was Eleanor Coade, junior (1733–1821). She is known as "Mrs" because that was the title for women in business, and so she often gets confused with her mother, who set up the company. However, Eleanor Coade did not marry until her 80s, and then it was only to allow her cousin to keep on the business. Her father, a wool finisher, went bankrupt and died, but Eleanor had, unusually for the time, managed to set up a business in her own name, so she wasn't brought down by his debts and was able to save her mother from destitution.

Eleanor was both a brilliant businesswoman and a very fine sculptor. She not only ran one of the most successful 18th-century companies, she also created many of the original sculptures from which the moulds were taken. She bought a pottery in Lambeth in London, on the site where the Royal Festival Hall now stands. For a while, she kept on the previous owner as manager, though she sacked him on discovering that he was claiming to be the brains behind the business.

When Eleanor died, aged 88 and extremely rich, she left money to many of her female relatives and friends, stipulating that they and not their husbands should have control of it. Her obituary even appeared in *The Gentleman's Magazine,* a rare honour for a woman.

It used to be thought that Eleanor took her secret Coade-stone recipe to her grave, but in recent years a few potters have managed to crack the formula. One of the first was the Portobello-based potter who helped restore Portobello's Coade stone pillars (see previous page) and made the mile markers that denote the underfoot distance along the Portobello promenade.

MORE COADE STONE IN EDINBURGH

Gosford House, Longniddry, Edinburgh EH32 0PY: Coade stone lions on the roof, restored by the same potter who recently restored Belmont, Mrs Coade's amazing Dorset house.

Assembly Rooms, 54 George Street, Edinburgh EH2 2LR: three Coade stone Vestal Virgins in the Crush Hall.

St Michael's Church, Inveresk, Edinburgh EH21 7UA: Major Norman Ramsay's sarcophagus, lying on top of a Coade stone cannon, sword and cannonballs.

Dalmeny House, South Queensferry, Edinburgh EH30 9TQ: ornamental Coade stone chimneys, battlements, plaques, coats of arms and pinnacles on the roof – listed by Coade stone expert Alison Kelly as "the most extensive Gothic Coade work surviving on a private house, costing £3,300, plus nearly £1,000 for packing".

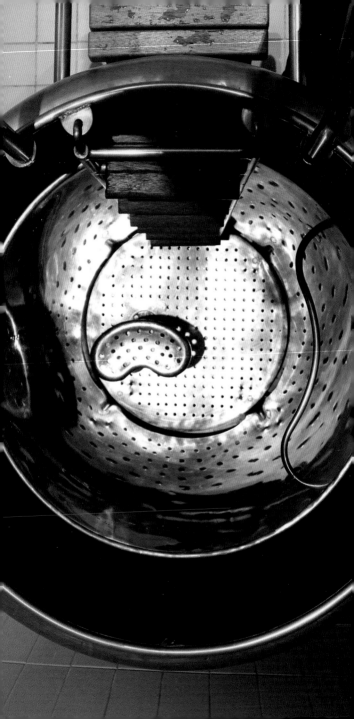

THE AEROTONE

Portobello Swim Centre, 57 The Promenade, Portobello, Edinburgh EH15 2BS
• www.edinburghleisure.co.uk/venues/portobello-swim-centre
• Open weekdays 7am–10pm, Sat 9am–4pm, Sun 9am–6pm
• Last Aerotone session starts 8.30pm. Booking advisable. £5.60 per 1-hr hire
• Buses: 15/15A, 26, 40

Victorian bubble therapy

Like a cross between a space capsule and a giant milk churn, the Aerotone at Portobello baths is a Victorian prototype jacuzzi, prized for its therapeutic qualities and as an aid for sports injuries. There are very few still in operation in the world – the only other one in Britain is in Manchester's Victoria Baths.

Portobello Baths were built in 1901 and prided themselves on being at the forefront of bathing technology. Edward VII used to bathe in the "Portobello ponds", as they were known, which had separate pools for men and women. In 1933 Scotland's first wave machine was added, and also an outdoor lido, its waters heated by the pipes of the local power station. And then in June 1939 a state-of-the-art Aeratone (over the years, its middle "a" has morphed into a more bubblesome "o") was installed.

The Aerotone Therapeutic Bath was developed by Professor William Oliver of the University of Edinburgh as "a powerful aid in the treatment of Circulatory and Rheumatic Diseases". The bath was originally manufactured and marketed by his company, Turbulyr Products Ltd, of West Harbour Road, Edinburgh. You can see how cutting-edge it was if you search Pathe's website for aeratone (www.britishpathe.com). The Aerotones became a favourite with footballers and an essential for sufferers of rheumatism – at one time, most hospitals, spas and sports clubs had one.

Nowadays half the swimmers at Portobello's beautiful council-run pool saunter past the last of the Aerotones on their way to their routine dip and don't even notice this extraordinary contraption. Go with a friend and take it in turns. Your friend stands at the Frankenstein control panel while you climb down into the capsule and sit nervously on the small bench inside, the water now up to your neck. Your friend then starts turning the knobs and levers to add bubbles and jets, setting off what seems like a gigantic underwater eruption. You will feel a strange mixture of being deeply refreshed, satisfyingly pummelled and slightly waterboarded. Well worth a fiver.

JOPPA ROCKS AND SALT PANS

Joppa Pans, Seaview Terrace, Edinburgh EH15 2HF
• www.edinburghgeolsoc.org
• Accessible 24 hrs but best viewed at low tide
• Free admission
• Bus: 26

Make sure you visit Joppa at low tide and wearing grippy shoes because the rocks can be slippery. There are steps down to the shoreline just east of the Rockville Inn, beyond where the buses turn. As you walk

Rocks between a hard place

west along the shore towards Portobello beach, you are stepping back through 20 million years, heading towards rocks which are 300 million years old.

This area is hugely important geologically and is full of fascinating patterns and evidence of the Earth's formation. They were studied by the influential geologist Hugh Miller, though it was perhaps his inability to reconcile this evidence of evolution with his religious beliefs that led him to shoot himself in his Portobello cottage on Christmas Eve 1856.

The rocks here were formed during the Carboniferous Period, when Scotland was close to the Equator and still part of the same landmass as Europe and North America. There was a shallow tropical sea full of marine organisms and coral, which turned into layers of fossils and limestone. The sea would cyclically recede, leaving a shallow freshwater lagoon in which lycopod trees grew (like mangrove swamps); they eventually decayed into peat and then into seams of coal.

These layers were initially laid down horizontally, but they got tipped over by massive tectonic movements, which pushed them up into ridges at a 45–60° angle. The ridges of coal are most visible at the east end, and are part of the same seam that was mined at Newcraighall Colliery from 1897 until 1968. Below the hotel you can also see twists of sandstone which are the remnants of sand from the side of rivers. See if you can find two lobe-like swirls of sandstone, below the most easterly corner of the street-level wall which starts at Rock Cottage. This is where wet sand sank into the mud before it had hardened.

The other fascinating thing about this area is that from 1630 until the 1950s it was used for salt panning – the harvesting of sea salt by evaporation in shallow rock pools, or "pans". Some salt workers lived in Rock Cottage, and the pans were in the now grassy area next to it. England had a salt tax, so cheaper Scottish salt was often smuggled over the border. And to keep production costs lower, the salters and their families were kept as slaves by the Earl of Abercorn, only stopped by the abolition of slavery in 1833. Leaves quite a salty taste …

NEWHAILES HOUSE

Newhailes, Musselburgh, Edinburgh EH21 6RY
• Tel: 0131 653 5599 • www.nts.org.uk/Property/Newhailes
• Email: newhailes@nts.org.uk • Estate open all year, daily, dawn to dusk
• Admission free • House: tours by appointment only, 12 noon–3.30pm
• Full tour: adult £12.50; concession £9.00; family £29.50; 1-parent
family £23.00 • Taster/family tour: adult £9.00; concession £6.50;
family £22.00; 1-parent family £17.00
• Buses: 30, 45

Enchanted woodlands

Newhailes House is a rather unusual National Trust of Scotland property because instead of restoring the 17th-century villa to its perceived former glory, the Trust chose to preserve it as it was when they took it on in 1997. This was mainly due to their experience with the House of Dun in Angus, which was so lavishly restored that it looked as if a Laurence Llewelyn-Bowen had run amok, playing fast and loose with period detail. By contrast, with its fading carpets and darkened paintwork, Newhailes seems to be auditioning for a role in *Sleeping Beauty*.

A walk through the grounds is equally enchanting, landscaped by Sir James Dalrymple and developed by his granddaughter, Christian. A lover of trees, she had a raised path built through the woods, the Ladies' Walk, allowing those long bustled skirts to swish through, unsnagged by undergrowth. Halfway along, you find the ruins of a shell grotto – atmospheric now, but when it was built it would have been a glittering fairy castle in the mists, perhaps competing with other nearby grottoes (see p. 258-261). The walls were impregnated with semi-precious stones, fragments of mirror and exotic shells. Opposite, an artificial waterfall cascaded into a pool, and as a finishing touch, smoke was piped theatrically through the grotto's walls.

A BLACK OBELISK FOR A COMPLEX MAN

At the end of the Ladies' Walk, you'll find the ruins of the 18th-century tea house, which strides the Brunstane Burn and allowed the ladies to recover from the strenuous fifteen-minute walk. If you still have energy, head back and up onto the slopes above the shell grotto, where in a woodland clearing, you will find a hidden black obelisk.

This monument was erected in 1746 by Sir James in honour of his cousin, John Dalrymple, 2nd Earl of Stair. Its Latin inscription details how the Earl, who fought in 1743 as second-in-command to George II at Dettingen, showed "superlative care and great good sense as King's envoy to France" and "procured good will and frustrated his enemies by design". Dalrymple seems to have been a complicated human being: aged 9, he accidentally shot his older brother and was exiled by his parents, who could not bear to see his face. And when his lover, Lady Eleanor Primrose Campbell, bruised by her violent first marriage, refused his proposal, he bribed a servant to let him into her bedroom and stood naked by her window over the High Street. Fearing the damage to her reputation, Lady Primrose finally accepted his hand. Enchanting.

JONAH AND THE WHALE MURAL

Musselburgh Sports Centre, 101 Newbigging, Musselburgh, Edinburgh
EH21 7AS
• Tel: 0131 653 5208
• Pool opening times vary and it's sometimes closed for private
functions, training, etc; call in advance to check

*Lustrous
locker
room treasure*

From the outside, Musselburgh swimming pool is not the most promising venue for an art gallery. Nor for that matter is the inside. The entire complex has a municipal, crowd-herding feel, albeit with a bit of a 1990s hexagonal spin. Push through the barriers and you'll see a fairly standard 25-metre council pool, large tinted windows, pleasant for a few lengths of crawl – but no artistic strokes. Glance left and still no art, just rows of poolside lockers and changing rooms.

But look again and you'll spot a strip of something glittering through the verticals of grey and beige. Swirls of copper, bronze and silvery blue rise and fall – their sweep across the back wall constantly interrupted by the lines of cubicles. Head through the other side of the changing area and you can get close up on this extraordinary lustre tile mosaic depicting Jonah's aquatic encounter. It's so vast it makes you want to step back and take in the whole picture. But you can't. The damned lockers are in the way!

So you'll have to make do with a frustratingly tight angle on this wonderful tiled mural. It seems crazy that something commissioned for the opening of the pool has ended up hidden from view. Margery Clinton, who died in 2005, was an important Scottish potter; she was born in Glasgow and based her pottery nearby in East Lothian. She dedicated her artistic career to working with reduction lustre glaze techniques – originally developed in medieval Islamic art – and used them to create darkly shimmering pots and tiles. Her work has been on display at Tate Britain, the V&A, the National Museum of Scotland, Glasgow Art Gallery … and at the back of Musselburgh swimming pool.

The story of Jonah, who was swallowed by a whale and then spewed out on God's orders, appears in the Hebrew Bible and the Quran, and so is the perfect subject matter both for a Middle Eastern tile technique and for a swimming pool so near the sea. Sadly, due to the corrosive effect of chlorine, some of the tiles have dropped off and been replaced by beige bathroom tiles. However, Clinton bequeathed her specialist reduction kiln and lustre recipes to her assistant and friend, potter Alison Robinson, who continues to research and develop her glaze techniques.

DOUBLE DYKES HEDGE

5 Double Dykes, Inveresk, Musselburgh EH21 7TF
• Viewable 24 hrs
• Free
• Buses: 26, 44, 30, 40

Hedge-box
zoo

There are two amazing hidden gardens in Inveresk: the National Trust-owned Inveresk Lodge Garden, with its parakeet-filled aviary and Edwardian glasshouses; and the Shepherd House Garden, with its elegant sculptural fountains and wonderful shell house (see p. 261). Both are beautifully created and maintained to the highest standards. But it's on a back lane of the village that you'll find a bit of amateur cultivation that will really bring a smile to your face.

About twenty-five years ago, Leonora Williamson was trimming the low privet hedge in her small front garden on Double Dykes, which leads from Inveresk Garden Lodge up to the Lewisvale Park. For some reason she thought, "I'll leave a few lumps" and went off to look for some guidance on the art of topiary. But she couldn't find anything, not even in the George IV Library. She decided she would give it a shot anyway. She had an idea for one lump: "You could make that into a dog." Another suggested a cat, the next maybe a train. And so she braced herself and started snipping freehand. She'd hoped her husband would do a lump or two, but he wasn't really interested. She wanted to make a Buddha but she couldn't get the legs or hands right, so that became a bear. Soon her hedge had quite a menagerie sitting on top.

Feeling a little foolish and wishing the hedge was out of view at the back of the house, Leonora cleared up and disappeared inside her cottage, thinking she'd made a terrible mistake and might have to cut off all the figures. But soon she heard the delighted laughter of children outside, and intense debate as to what each one was. People started complimenting her on her dolphin, her rabbit, her duck … but the confusion didn't deter her, it just inspired her to keep on snipping. Each year the sculptures got bigger, denser, more elaborate. And they started to evolve. A helping hand accidentally cut the tail off her cat, so that became a pig. What was initially a truck morphed into an elephant, with a wire to support its trunk. She's currently growing it some legs. Leonora reckons anyone with a hedge can do it: just take a deep breath and grab those secateurs. You never know what might leap out.

HOFFMAN KILN

Prestongrange Museum
Morison's Haven, Prestonpans, East Lothian, EH32 9RX
• Tel: 0131 653 2904 (April–Sept)
• www.prestongrange.org
• Open-air site. Admission free. Self-guided tours using a mobile phone
Visitor centre & café open daily 1 April–30 Sept: 11.30am–4.30pm
• Buses: 26 (Lothian), 128 (Eves Coaches)

Ring of fire

The Hoffman Continuous Kiln sits opposite the entrance to the Prestongrange Museum's visitor centre, high up on a bank, making its 33.5-metre-high chimney seem even more vertiginous. Looking like a cross between a fortified labyrinth and a giant train depot, the main body of the building seems squat by comparison, but on approach you realise how vast it is. A giant drive-in kiln, built in 1937 from the very product it created: bricks.

The kiln's design, patented by German engineer Friedrich Hoffmann in 1858, is remarkably ingenious. It makes super-efficient use of materials and energy, and allows for stacks of bricks to be continually fired on rotation through its ring of adjoining kiln chambers: while one batch is being loaded, the next is firing, the next cooling down, the next being emptied and the next loaded. Each of the 24 chambers could fire 11,000 bricks, formed out of a mix of clay and shale, or "blaes". Because shale is rich in combustible oil, the heated air channelled from the neighbouring chamber was enough to ignite it. The residual heat from the kilns was also channelled out to underground heating for the wet clay bricks to dry out before firing.

For a long time, the bricks were hand-pressed into individual moulds, marked with the PG or Preston Grange indent. The kilns were also used to fire other heavy ceramics like tiles and water pipes, roughly glazed with salt. Not only was the kiln efficient, it was perfectly located to gather the materials it needed locally. The coal and shale came from the colliery next door, the clay was dug from a seam just along the road at the Upper Birslie Plantation, sand for dusting the brick moulds came from the shore and salt was gathered from the salt pans down at Prestonpans and Joppa (see p. 247). Morrison's haven, a harbour which used to nestle in the coast right here, meant that the products could be shipped around the world.

When Prestongrange Colliery closed in 1962, the increased cost of transporting raw materials to the brickworks made it uneconomic: the fires were gradually dampened down until they were extinguished in 1975. You used to be able to walk into the kiln and explore its amazing vaults, but lack of funds means that the building is gradually reverting into the earth from which it was formed. Hopefully it can be saved from the fate of the ones in Armadale Fife, which were demolished in 2012.

Masie Aitchesoun	Janet Boyd
Mergarett Aitchesoun	Bessie Broune
Agnes Aird	Thomas Brounhill
Marjorie Andersone	Wife of Thomas Brounhill
Margaret Auchinmoutie	Duncan Buchquhannan
Marioun Bailzie	Margaret Butter
Christian Blaikie	Martha Butter
Meg Bogtoun	Jonett Campbell
"The people who sat in darkness saw great light"	

WITCHES' MEMORIALS

The Prestoungrange Gothenburg, 227 High Street, Prestonpans, EH32 9BE
• Tel: 01875 819922
• www.thegoth.co.uk
• Admission free
• Phone day before to check access

Cuthill Park, Prestoungrange Road, Prestonpans, East Lothian, EH32 9SE

> *Scotland's Salem*

The back garden of the Gothenburg pub has an installation commemorating the eighty women and one man executed for witchcraft in Prestonpans.

The 16th- and 17th-century persecution of those deemed to be witches had its epicentre in East Lothian, and the Prestoungrange court was particularly vigilant. Those under suspicion were mainly women: they had usually done little wrong other than being a midwife, offering herbal cures, being poor and widowed, or suffering from what we now term dementia. For a pre-Enlightenment, highly religious society that believed in the devil, witchcraft could explain everything from bad weather to erectile dysfunction. Around 4,500 Scots were executed for witchcraft – Scottish historian Roy Pugh has called this a mini-holocaust.

The first epidemic kicked off in 1589, when King James VI of Scotland was convinced that the storms preventing his bride (Princess Anne of Denmark) from sailing over from Oslo and consummating their marriage were being conjured up by a coven of witches, in league with his enemy, the Earl of Bothwell. Agnes Sampson (a midwife from Humbie), Geillis Duncan (a maidservant from Tranent) and Dr John Fian (a Prestonpans teacher) were all personally "questioned" by James VI, found guilty and executed.

Women suspected of witchcraft were tested by a "witch pricker", who would strip the defendant naked, shave her and stick a pin into her somewhere tender: if no blood was drawn, then she was guilty. Unfortunately, the professional prickers, like John Kincaird of Tranent, were paid by the number of confessions obtained, and so would use sleight of hand to get a bloodless result. The woman would then be tortured into confessing and naming other witches – who would undergo the same treatment, so a cascade of women were tortured with terrible contraptions, like the witches' bradle (bradawl), which forced iron spikes into their mouths. Alternatively, they could be douked 'til they drowned in the Nor'loch, or strangled and burnt in front of the assembled crowds.

In 2004 the Baron of Prestoungrange conducted an "absolute pardoning" of the eighty-one women found guilty in Prestonpans. Andrew Crummy and Tom Ewing created the murals behind the Gothenburg and also those in Cuthill Park. There are many other exhibits relating to the witches inside the Goth. An annual commemoration is held at Halloween, alongside a week of arts events with performances by storyteller Ros Parkin and plays by Roy Pugh.

LAVA GROTTO

Cockenzie House and Gardens
22 Edinburgh Road, Cockenzie; and Port Seton, Edinburgh EH32 0HY
• Tel: 01875 819 456 • www.cockenziehouseandgardens.com
• Email: info@cockenziehouseandgardens.co.uk
• Admission to gardens free; check website for opening times
• Bus: 26 (only buses going to Seton Sands or Port Seton). Eves Coaches:
128, 129

Lava palaver

The grotto at the foot of Cockenzie House gardens has the same coronet-like peaks as the boathouse at Gosford House, but it's very unusual as it's made out of lumps of pumice-like lava. The dramatic gothic arched doorway is made from a whale's jawbone. Inside, if you peer past the Santa stuff (he rents the place out at Christmas), you can see that the walls are lined with faded shells – now almost a black and white photograph of what once was. Shells you can understand: they're everywhere. Whales' jawbones: there's a few around. But lava? There hasn't been an active volcano in Scotland for – ooh – 55 million years?

Well, Cockenzie House was owned by the Cadell family, who before founding their fortunes in iron, were panning them in salt. They sold a lot of the salt to Iceland (the country, not the supermarket chain) for preserving their fish. Why a sea-locked island needed to shop so far for their salt is a mystery – but when the ships headed back to Cockenzie harbour, they would fill their holds with rock for ballast. That rock was lava, from Iceland's most active volcano, Hekla. And so, lumpily written across the front of the grotto in porous rock, is the alternative spelling: "Hecla". Which in turn inspired the name of the art gallery that Yvonne Murphy and Gillian Hart set up inside Cockenzie House. Other interesting things to be found inside the house include a collection of early photographs from around 1855, taken by Sir Robert Cadell, who as well as being a general in the Crimean War, was experimenting in photography along with pioneers Hill and Adamson. One of them shows Hecla back in its early

days. There are artists' studios at the back, many of their wares on sale in the shop. The garden has allotments and two turreted "Claret" towers built into the original walls.

Despite all the efforts of the local community, Cockenzie House is sadly under threat of being turned into a care home. But whatever happens, the house, walls and features are A-Listed, so Hecla will endure.

There's a very fine secret garden café hidden in a high terrace conservatory overlooking the sea, run by Edinburgh's favourite German konditormeister, Falko.

GOSFORD DOUBLE GROTTOES

Gosford House Grounds, Longniddry, East Lothian, Edinburgh EH32 0PY
- Tel: 01875 870808
- www.gosfordhouse.co.uk
- Email: rob@gosfordhouse.co.uk
- Open Easter and summer. See website for details

Random rubble

Robert Adams designed two grottoes for the grounds of Gosford House, built at the end of the 18th century. One is the Ice House, built into a grassy bank, blending into the glorious landscaped garden, and allowing the kitchens of the big house to store ice for syllabubs and slicing ham. The other is a curling house, the front curved wall rising to peaks like a crown, enveloping its store of winter sport curling stones. Both grottoes are made out of what is described on the listed buildings site as "random rubble". Apologies due to Tammy Christison, the celebrated Aberlady stonemason who created them both. He painstakingly assembled different stones to create the rustic, natural effect, much of it *tufa* – a fluvial limestone riddled with holes as though a stone-worm has eaten through it, and favoured by the Etruscans and the Romans for their temples.

See overleaf for more glorious grottos.

GLORIOUS GARDEN GROTTOES

The word grotto, meaning cavern, often decorative and man-made, comes from the Old Italian *grotta*, which in turn derives from the Latin *crypta* and the Greek *krypte,* meaning hidden place. And it was on their tours of Italy and Greece that 18th-century grand homeowners were charmed by these little temples which had been built around caves and cascading water, elegantly decorated with stone or shell mosaics, and guarded by statues of deities to ward off any cave-dwelling evil spirits. "Oh, darling," they said, "let's have one of them back home in the garden."

Their architects promptly conjured up the most romantic follies, attempting to imitate nature by using rough stones and porous rocks. But then competition kicked in. They added lumps of glass, shells, semi-precious stones, and at Newhailes House (see p. 249), dry ice for that "grotto in the mist" effect. Fortunes were spent. Over 200 years later, the bling has gone and the shells have faded, but a few of the precious little hideaways still stand. And they have inspired some recent interpretations. Opposite are some latter- and modern-day examples to compete for your attention.

Lava Grotto: 19th-century glass plate negative by General Sir Robert Cadell.

Shell house

Shepherd House Garden, Inveresk, Midlothian, Edinburgh EH21 7TH

- Tel: 0131 665 2570
- www.shepherdhousegarden.co.uk
- Email: ann@shepherdhousegarden.co.uk
- Open infrequently: check website for opening times
- Admission: £5
- Buses: 26, 44, 30, 40

As a child, Lady Ann Fraser always loved shells and decided that what Shepherd House Garden needed was a shell house, a bit like the Queen Mother's Memorial one, which you can find in the Royal Botanic Gardens. As Lady Ann lived just outside Musselburgh, there were bound to be plenty of seashells to plunder. In 2013 the family had a house built specially and invited a bunch of art students to help decorate the interior with boxes and boxes of scallops, limpets and mussel shells, which were painstakingly stuck on with tile cement. The results are spectacular – different shades of mussel shell form a chequered border with lines of allium flowers, which Ann did herself. On top is a golden flying-duck weather vane, a homage to the roof resident of the shed that once stood here, a wild mallard who used to hatch out her annual clutch of ducklings and then demand an escort to the river.

"The Light Pours Out Of Me"

Jupiter Artland, Wilkieston, Edinburgh EH27 8BB

- Tel: 01506 889900
- www.jupiterartland.org
- Email: enquiries@jupiterartland.org
- Open May–Sept
- Admission: adult £8.50; child £4.50; family (2+2) £23.50; (2+4) £31.50; OAP £6.00; student £4.50; under 6s & disabled badge holders: free
- Buses [First]: 27, X27. See website for directions. (NB do not use postcode for Sat Navs)

In the wonderful Jupiter Artland, the artist Anya Gallaccio has built a modern-day grotto which captures the impact that 18th-century grottoes must have had on their audiences. "The Light Pours Out Of Me" is cut into the forest earth. Behind a golden barbed-wire fence is a slot down which you descend into a glittering cave lined with amethyst and obsidian. Apart from the sheer decadence of it, Gallaccio was interested in the hippy California crystal lore. Amethyst is thought to have healing powers for all kinds of ailments, from bereavement to financial loss. Black volcanic obsidian cleanses negative psychic smog from your aura. But on a more scientific level, it's very, very shiny.

TOPIARY HEADS

Address: somewhere...

> **Yew'll
> be sorry ...**

Somewhere near Edinburgh, three giant topiary heads glare out at passers-by: a Roman centurion, a Navaho tribesman and an Easter Island Polynesian, carved from three ancient yew trees. If you step too close to them, their eyes light up a fiery red, warning you away.

Unfortunately, people who spot them often hang out taking selfies, walk where they're clearly not meant to, and leave behind all sorts of unpleasant detritus. Each morning, the owners have to spend a good hour cleaning up rubbish. The road is closed to public traffic, but still people think, "It's only me", and drive up. If this keeps happening, the owners will be forced to take drastic measures ... perhaps even decapitation.

So please, if you discover the location of the heads and want to visit, don't drive up there. Park on the public road, approach quietly on foot and maybe even take away any litter you find. Those heads are in your hands ...

ALPHABETICAL INDEX

ALPHABETICAL INDEX

Acknowledgements

Special secret thanks to Rachel Howard, Susanna Beaumont, Colin McLaren, Lila Rawlings, Conrad Molleson, Lesley Pearson, Ima Jackson, Morris Paton, Barbara Gillespie, Frances O'Neill, Miles Tubb, George Lamb, Sasha Callaghan, Robin Mainstone, Barry Edmonds, Iain Campbell, Kenneth Williamson, Margaret Swindale, Gillian McCay, Tracy Smith, John Arthur, Morvern Cunningham, Barbara Harvie, John Stewart, Robert Cooper, The Art of It, The Cockburn Society, Edinburgh World Heritage and above all to my amazing mother, Alison Robinson, for her endless help, expertise and enthusiasm.

Photography credits:

All photographs by **Oscar Van Heek** except
Book Sculptures: Photograph by Chris Scott
Blair Street Vaults: Photograph courtesy of Mercat Tours
Lava Grotto glass plate negative by General Sir Robert Cadell, and modern photograph by Sheila Ritchie, both courtesy of the Cockenzie House and Gardens Trust

Maps **Cyrille Suss** - Layout design: **Roland Deloi** - Layout: **Stéphanie Benoit** - Proofreading: **Jana Gough** and **Kimberly Bess**

© JONGLEZ 2016
Registration of copyright: May 2016 – Edition: 01
ISBN: 978-2-36195-148-1
Printed in Bulgaria by Multiprint